How
YOU™
are
like
Shampoo
For JOB SEEKERS

Praise from around the world for
How YOU™ Are Like Shampoo For Job Seekers

"The reality of a global pool of talent means heightened competitiveness for every job. *How YOU™ Are Like Shampoo For Job Seekers* provides a step-by-step plan for ensuring the most important brand— you!— is positioned to win in the marketplace."
> — James M. Lafferty, President and General Manager
> Procter & Gamble Philippines

"As an HR professional with many years of experience, some of the best advice I can give any potential job seeker is to understand who you are, what you want from your next job, and how to sell that to a potential employer. Brenda Bence's book will help you do just that! I strongly urge you to read *How YOU™ Are Like Shampoo for Job Seekers* as the first step in your next job search. The proof will be in the results."
> — Dalia Turner, Microsoft Asia Pacific
> High Potential Program Manager

"Excellent interviewing skills and a stellar resume can only get you so far. Today, you need a dynamic personal brand to obtain a job that will fulfill you and bring you the kind of income you deserve. *How YOU™ Are Like Shampoo for Job Seekers* is quite simply the definitive roadmap to job search success through the power of personal branding."
> — Nora Bammann, Human Resources, The Kroger Company

"Bence is a proven marketer and has translated her outstanding grasp of product branding into valuable lessons that can be applied to job seekers as they market and develop themselves."
> — Steve Golsby, CEO, Mead Johnson Nutrition

"You may have a great resume, and you may interview well. But that won't be enough to compete against job hunters who have taken the time to define and communicate a powerful personal brand. In *How YOU™ Are Like Shampoo for Job Seekers*, Brenda Bence shows you how to use personal branding to gain the edge over others vying for the same job. It's a great 'how to' manual for a successful job search!"
> — Gary Woollacott, CEO, Opus Executive Search

"In a warm, insightful, and pragmatic style, Bence shows you how to use every advantage and strength at your disposal to create a memorable personal brand that can propel you to the top of a company's 'want' list. If you want to prosper in today's competitive job market, this book is your ticket!"
> — Anders Lundquist, President
> Pacific 2000, International Recruitments

A Personal Note from the Author

I am proud to announce support for Dress for Success®, an international organization whose mission is "to promote the economic independence of disadvantaged women by providing professional attire, a network of support, and the career development tools to help women thrive in work and in life." By way of support for this strong cause, my husband, Daniel, and I will donate $1.00 to Dress for Success for every copy sold of the *How YOU™ are like Shampoo* book series.

I believe strongly in the mission of Dress for Success and, through this partnership, we know we are empowering disadvantaged women to take charge of their lives and careers. Many thanks to you for your purchase of *How YOU™ are like Shampoo for Job Seekers*. By doing so, you have made a difference in the lives of thousands of women, and we are grateful to you for helping us to support such a purposeful organization.

To find out more about Dress for Success, please visit www.dressforsuccess.org.

How
YOU™
are
like
Shampoo

For JOB SEEKERS

The Proven **Personal Branding System**
To Help You Succeed In Any Interview And
Secure the Job of Your Dreams

Brenda Bence

BRANDING EXPERT AND EXECUTIVE COACH

Published by Global Insight Communications LLC, Las Vegas, Nevada, U.S.A.

ISBN: 978-0-9799010-5-8
Library of Congress Control Number: 2008935844

Cover design by George Foster, Foster Covers (www.fostercovers.com)
Front cover photography by Kurt Heck (www.kurtheck.com)
Graphic design by Jay Cotton, Hot Ant Design (www.hotant.com.au)
Cartoons by Brenda Brown (http://webtoon.com)
Interior design and typesetting by Eric Myhr

The stories in this book are based on real events and real people. Where requested, and in order to protect the privacy of certain individuals, names and identifying details have been changed.

Publisher's Cataloging-in-Publication Data:

Bence, Brenda S.
  How you are like shampoo for job seekers: the proven personal branding system to help you succeed in any interview and secure the job of your dreams / Brenda S. Bence.
  p. cm.
  ISBN 978-0-9799010-5-8
1. Job Hunting. 2. Vocational guidance. 3. Career development. 4. Branding (marketing) I. Title.
HF5382.75.U6 B46 2009
650.14 20--dc22   2008935844

To my mother, Pearl Myers-Bence,
my very first 'life coach'

and

To my job-seeker coaching clients
who allowed me to travel along with them
on their journeys of discovery

Contents

Preface   11

Introduction: Your Job Search — How *Are* YOU™ Like Shampoo?   17

The Power of Brands   23

Step 1: Define It

Defining Your Personal Brand   31

Element #1: *Audience*   39

Element #2: *Need*   59

Element #3: *Comparison*   71

Element #4: *Unique Strengths*   83

Element #5: *Reasons Why*   99

Element #6: *Brand Character*   111

Pulling It All Together   125

Step 2: Communicate It

Taking YOU™ on Interviews   141

Launching Your Job-Seeker Personal Brand   145

Activity #1: *Actions*   153

Activity #2: *Reactions*   171

Activity #3: *Look*   185

Activity #4: *Sound*   201

Activity #5: *Thoughts*   217

Your Complete Job-Seeker Personal Brand Marketing Plan   235

Step 3: Avoid Damaging It

Job-Seeker Personal Brand Busters™   243

Quiz: The Top 20 Job-Seeker Personal Brand Busters™   247

Assuring Long-Term Success   263

Appendix A: *Great Interview Questions for YOU™*   267

Appendix B: *Personality Profiles and Tests*   270

Suggested Books   272

About the Author   273

Acknowledgments   275

Contact Information   277

Preface

Each one of us has a fire in our heart for something. It's our goal in life to find it and to keep it lit.

— Mary Lou Retton, Olympic Gold Medal Gymnast

I just might be the kind of person you love to hate. Why? Well, I wake up every single morning happy, with a smile on my face. I can't wait to get out of bed and head off to work. I thoroughly enjoy what I do for a living. And because I'm so satisfied in my professional life, this rolls over into the rest of my life. I have a wonderful marriage, loving relationships with family, terrific friends, an active social life … and the list goes on and on.

Here's the funny part: Early on in my career, I just naturally thought everyone else felt the same way as me! But then, I realized not everyone in the big corporations where I worked was as happy as I was. I also did some research and read studies that showed that as many as 75% of all people are miserable in their jobs. And, finally, through my professional coaching practice, I discovered a lot of my clients were unhappy in their work, too.

All of this really troubled me. If you're unhappy with what you do for a living — where you spend about one-half of your waking hours — how can you lead a full, productive, and complete life? If you're not happy in such a key aspect of your life as your work, how can you be completely fulfilled in the remaining hours? I knew something was wrong with this picture, and I began to think about what part I could play in helping to change that.

Think about it for a minute: What would the world be like if everyone loved their work as much as I do? We would be more content, more satisfied at work, and more fulfilled as a whole. As a result, our relationships would be better, and our family lives would be happier. What a difference it would make.

Maybe you're thinking, "Give me a break—that's a pipe dream!" But why not? If I can do it, why can't everybody else? Why can't you? I fundamentally believe we're all entitled to that kind of work fulfillment.

It has become a dream of mine that everybody should be genuinely happy and fulfilled at work. This includes you—finding yourself not only in a good job, but in a *great* job. This kind of life *is* within your reach. It just takes a bit of effort to achieve it. And that's where *How YOU™ are like Shampoo for Job Seekers* comes in.

I created the *How YOU™ are like Shampoo* series of personal branding books with this dream in mind. Based on the personal branding system that I have used for years with my professional and executive coaching clients, I have witnessed firsthand how powerful this personal branding process can be. So, a while back, I decided to put the system down on paper to be able to share it with more people. Then, I customized the system to work for job seekers like you who are ready to put job dissatisfaction behind you and find a job you truly love.

So, Who Am I Anyway?

You already know that I have spent quite a few years coaching clients to develop their personal brands. But let me share a little bit more about me and how I came to write the *How YOU™ are like Shampoo* personal branding book series.

In addition to working as a professional coach, I'm also an international branding and marketing trainer and professional speaker. Coaching and branding for corporations and individuals across the world has allowed me the wonderful fortune of living in, working in, and visiting almost 70 countries. As a result, I've met thousands of people from various walks of life all around the globe.

What is my main observation after meeting so many "different" kinds of people? That we are all fundamentally the same. From Switzerland to Sri Lanka to South Africa, we all ultimately want the same things: To earn a good living, enjoy our work, stay healthy, have a happy family life, enjoy meaningful friendships, and ultimately make a difference in some way.

So, if we're all alike, why would I write a series of books about *personal* branding? Because while we're all fundamentally the same, we also each have specific gifts and talents that are as unique to us as our individual DNA. It's a bit of a paradox, isn't it? We're the same, and yet, we're unique. And it's up to each of us to learn how to use our specific gifts and talents to make our lives and careers the best they can be — to make that difference in the world that we hope for. This is where personal branding comes in.

You've heard of serial killers? Well, think of me as a "serial brander" — I just can't stop branding! As a name brand marketer, I have worked for Procter & Gamble and Bristol-Myers Squibb on four different continents, where I was fortunate enough to manage many well-known brands like Pantene, Head & Shoulders, Vidal Sassoon, Ariel, Cheer, and Enfamil.

I spent years defining, launching, and building brands all around the world using an established process and framework that name-brand marketers have used for a long time to craft and communicate brands. You may not have known that such a process exists, but trust me: Great brands don't become great brands by accident! It's only because of a powerful process put into place by good, strategic marketers that these brands make millions. And it's only because of this process that successful brands continue to survive and thrive through economic ups and downs.

A few years ago, when I began actively coaching people to reach their goals and develop their individual personal brands, I started to experiment and apply these same principles of corporate branding to personal branding. I took the elements and framework used by name brand marketers and adjusted them to fit personal brands, so that all of us — as individuals — could thrive in our careers the same way those great name brands that you love so much have thrived in the market. Over time, I perfected this approach until it evolved into the unique personal branding system I'm about to share with you in this book — a system that walks you through the process of building your personal brand step by step by step, helping you to craft and effectively communicate YOU™. That's right — the trademarked *you*.

Today, you — or YOU™ — can apply the same system in your job search that big-company marketers have used for years to build enormously successful corporate brands. Can you see now "how YOU™

are like shampoo?" Just as a corporate marketer uses this proven process to build the mega-brand of a shampoo like Pantene or Vidal Sassoon or Head & Shoulders, you, too, will build the brand of YOU™.

Taking the Mystery Out of Personal Branding

Since the advent of personal branding about ten years ago, several books have been written on the subject. What makes *How YOU™ are like Shampoo for Job Seekers* different is that it offers you a complete system that covers every possible aspect of how to use personal branding to sail through your job search with a successful result — the job you want. This book goes beyond the various theories that surround personal branding to bring you practical, tangible tools for your brand that you can apply immediately as you look for the best possible job.

My hope is that this book will:

- Open yourself up to the power that comes from successfully branding you.
- Show you how your job search can not only be manageable, but can actually be energizing and fun.
- Expand your vision of the kind of job and career you deserve and are capable of achieving.
- Offer you empowering tips and tools you can use before, during, and after your interviews so that you'll feel confident and fully ready to wow your interviewers.
- Bring you the kind of career enhancement you have always wanted but weren't sure how to get.
- Put more money in your pocket when it's time to sign on the dotted line for that great new job.
- Give you the satisfaction of knowing you're reaching your full potential and living the gratifying, happy life that will put a smile on *your* face every morning.

It's exciting for me to share with you my personal branding system customized specifically for job seekers looking for a new, fulfilling position. I hope you'll have fun with it, too, as we move through this process together.

"*Today, you — or YOU™ — can apply the same system in your job search that big-company marketers have used for years to build enormously successful corporate brands.*

*Can you see now
'how YOU™are like shampoo?'*"

The Proven Pathway to Getting YOU™ a Great Job

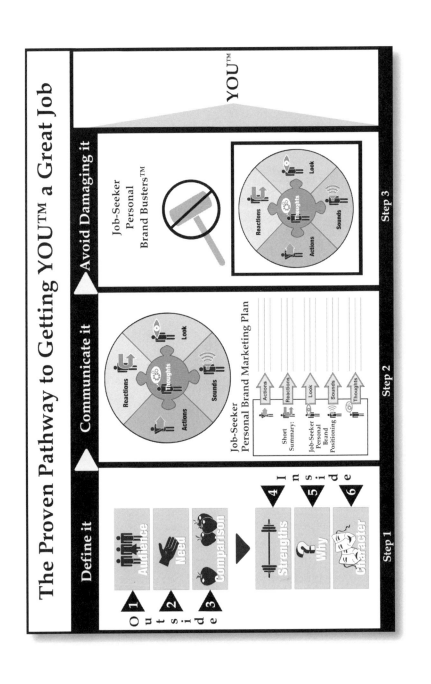

Introduction

Your Job Search— How *Are* You™ Like Shampoo?

It's better to look ahead and prepare than to look back and regret.

— Jackie Joyner-Kersee, Olympic Gold Medalist

Alfred Nobel was a very successful and wealthy Swedish industrialist in the late 1800's. He was widely credited with inventing two things: dynamite and the detonator, the apparatus that causes dynamite to ignite from a distance. He had made millions with these inventions, and he was living a wonderful millionaire's life.

His brother, Ludwig Nobel, who was also a well-known wealthy businessman, died in 1888. The obituary that showed up the next day in the newspaper, however, was switched, and it was *Alfred's* obituary that appeared, not Ludwig's. So, Alfred Nobel had the rare opportunity of opening up the morning paper and reading his own life story.

Can you imagine how powerful that would be?

But Alfred must have cringed when he read the headline of his obituary. It labeled Alfred "The Merchant of Death" because of his work with dynamite and detonators. He realized in that single moment that everything he had done would forever associate his personal brand with death — unless he took control and did something about it.

So, he decided to change his personal brand. He made a plan to develop the Nobel Prizes for five topics he really cared about — Physics, Chemistry, Medicine, Literature, and Peace. When he died in 1895, Alfred Nobel left the bulk of his millions to the establishment of those prizes. He didn't want his name, "Nobel," to stand for destruction and death. And look what the name Nobel stands for today — the most prestigious prizes awarded for outstanding achievements in those five important categories.

You've no doubt heard of the Nobel Prizes, right? But you probably didn't know the other work that Nobel had done in his life. That's because Alfred Nobel was successful in changing his personal brand so that his name could stand for what he wanted it to stand for.

You can change what you stand for, too, by creating your own personal brand and using it to invigorate your job search. As author Carl Bard said, "Though no one can go back and make a brand-new start, anyone can start from now and make a brand-new ending."

Did You Know You Already Have a Personal Brand?

When I speak to individuals or corporate groups about the topic of personal branding, occasionally someone will say, "Oh, that sounds interesting, but no thanks. I'm actually not into *self-promotion*. I don't have — or even want — a personal brand."

It's then that I break the news to them: **You already have a personal brand** (even if you haven't done anything as earth-shattering as invent dynamite!).

Yes, it's true. To have a personal brand, you don't have to be an inventor or even sit down and give your personal brand any thought. Just by virtue of being *you* in an interview or in your current workplace, you have a personal brand. The question is whether you have the personal brand you *want*. If not, you're leaving a lot more of your job search to chance than necessary. But fortunately, just like Alfred Nobel, you have the power to change your personal brand.

The bottom line is: If you don't take control of your job-seeker personal brand and make a conscious decision about how you want to come across in interviews, you may be leaving an impression that undermines your success.

Personal Branding and Your Job Search

Whether you're someone who wants out of a dead-end job or you're someone who has been out of a job for a while, defining your job-seeker personal brand can be the missing link to helping you find the kind of work you've been daydreaming about. Knowing who YOU™ are — the trademarked you — will give you renewed confidence and a clear edge in your job search. In fact, once you carefully define the job-seeker personal brand you want to communicate in interviews, you will be able to look at your job search with new meaning. It will help make every moment of your job hunt count. (And, yes, even though it's hard to believe — you may actually begin to find interviews fun.)

The ultimate goal of this book is to eliminate once and for all that groan you emit when the alarm goes off in the morning (you know the one we're talking about). I want you to be in a job that keeps you happy, fulfilled, and motivated.

But it really is up to you. If you want a better job, a successful career, and a more satisfying work life, you have to do something about it. Otherwise, nothing will happen. I can almost hear you saying, "But Brenda, I have no control over whether an interviewer likes me or not. If they decide not to hire me, what can I do?" Even though it may feel as though your job search is at the mercy of employers, a significant part of your job search success *is* in your control, and the foundation of that control is learning how to master your job-seeker personal brand. In *How YOU™ are like Shampoo for Job Seekers,* we will focus on the key parts of your job search that *are* in your control.

My Personal Branding System

So, let's recap. Here's the reality: You already have a job-seeker personal brand. Every time you have gone on an interview, you've presented that personal brand, maybe even without knowing it. Now, it's time to take control and learn how to manage it, leading to better success in the interview process and — ultimately — landing a great job.

How YOU™ are like Shampoo for Job Seekers is a do-it-yourself, no-nonsense guide to getting the job you want through successful personal branding. It's simple, easy to read, and it works. I have designed the personal branding system in this book to take the guesswork out of figuring out your job-seeker personal brand and how to use it to help you get the job you really want. It's all about practical application. Through an innovative, proven step-by-step process which utilizes exercises and worksheets, you will define a powerful job-seeker personal brand.

Most importantly, your brand won't just remain a nice idea in your head. After all, it would make no sense to spend time defining your brand and then just leave it in a desk drawer while you continue on the same as always, right?

No, you need a roadmap to help you communicate your brand to potential employers so that it serves you well. This is how you find that dream job you've always wanted. This is how you take the steering wheel of your career and drive it where you want it to go.

Through reading this book, you'll learn specific ways to communicate your brand to potential employers before, during, and after your interviews. We will work together to:

- Define your personal brand using a Job-Seeker Personal Brand Positioning Statement format modeled off the six core elements used by the most successful name brands in the world.

- Communicate your personal brand through a Job-Seeker Personal Brand Marketing Plan so that potential employers will see you as you *want* to be seen. This will help you effectively master the five activities you do throughout your job search that most impact your personal brand and your ability to get the job you want.

- Avoid damaging your job-seeker personal brand by learning from the mistakes others have made in the job search process. This is one of the most unique and fun parts of the system — our top 20 most damaging Job-Seeker Personal Brand Busters™. These will help you bypass the most common pitfalls others have experienced while hunting for a job. In other words, you'll know what to watch out for before you even get there!

- You will hear the input of dozens of recruiters and human resources experts that I have interviewed for this book. They've been in the trenches and seen it all!

- We'll use the graphic labeled "The Proven Pathway to Getting YOU™ a Great Job" on page 16. It serves as a map to explain each step of our personal branding system. Don't worry if it doesn't make sense to you yet. It will — I promise.

As you read these pages, I hope that you will experience that "ah-ha!" moment that comes from the power of thinking of yourself as a unique personal brand. I hope you'll see how you can use personal branding to make real changes in your life that can lead to a better job with increased income, job satisfaction, and exciting career progress.

Input Equals Output

How YOU™ are like Shampoo for Job Seekers is an interactive, action-oriented experience, but your job-seeker personal brand won't be handed to you on a silver platter. I can guarantee you one thing for sure: What you put *in* to defining and communicating your job-seeker personal brand is exactly what you will get *out* of it. The more time and energy you devote to this process, the faster you will get the job you want.

Get ready to feel empowered as you take charge of your job-seeker personal brand and become the Brand Manager of YOU™. Let's discover how to help you get the job that will fulfill you for years to come.

"This is our best-selling brand!"

$$\boxed{1}$$

The Power of Brands

A brand is a living entity — and it is enriched or undermined cumulatively over time, the product of a thousand small gestures.

— Michael Eisner, Former CEO of Disney

No book on personal branding would be complete without an understanding of the powerful and influential role that brands play in our lives every day. In 2001, *Time* magazine reported that the average American citizen sees an estimated 3,000 brands per day. When I first read that statistic, I couldn't believe it! But I suspect that number — which is almost certainly even larger today — holds true for anyone living and working in a large city anywhere in the world. In fact, the proof is right in front of me when I walk down a street in Shanghai and look at all of the signs ... when I ride in my car from my home in Bangkok to the airport with hundreds of billboards lining the way ... when I walk down a supermarket aisle in Dubai or London and see the myriad of brands peering down at me.

Think about it for a moment. How many brands have *you* seen today on product labels, the side of a bus, the top of a taxicab, or in the newspaper? Everywhere you look, brand names are screaming for your attention. Let's face it: Brands are everywhere and are such a part of our day-to-day modern lives that we may not even think about them.

But out of those 3,000 brands you encounter every day, if you're like most people, you will probably be faithful to at least one or two brands throughout most of your life. Are you loyal to a favorite brand? Would you consider it out of the question, for example, to wear anything but

Adidas tennis shoes or to switch from your favorite brand of shaving cream? Why? What is the allure of that favorite brand of yours? What does it offer you that no other brand can? Great brands build intense loyalty with the people who buy them.

Brands can be incredibly big and influential, too. Take Coca-Cola as an example. The company sells an estimated $15 billion of Coke per year — more than $1 billion *per month*. At the time of this writing, that's more than the gross domestic product of around 85 countries in the world. How's *that* for powerful?

The Untouchables

So, what do we know so far? We know that brands are everywhere, that they can create intense loyalty in us, and that they are big and influential. Is there any question why I find brands so fascinating?

But what's even more amazing about brands is that they have all of this power and influence, yet … you cannot touch a brand. It's true! You can smell the aroma of a Starbucks cup of coffee, you can taste the kick of a Mentos when you pop it in your mouth, you can hear the Nokia phone ring tone, you can feel the wet aluminum of an ice cold can of Pepsi in your hand, and you can see the golden arches of the McDonald's logo, but you cannot *touch* a brand. The smell, touch, or sight of a product is really only just a representation of that brand. The brand itself is actually intangible. Its power exists only in your mind.

So, can these intangible things called "brands" actually influence the way we act and think?

Powerful Brand Images

Great brands are like people. They have a personality and a character all their own. Stop for a moment, look around you, and find two doorways that you can see from where you are. In the first doorway, imagine that Mercedes Benz — the brand — is standing there as a *person* (not the car, but the brand of Mercedes Benz itself). What kind of person would the Mercedes Benz brand be? Is it a man or a woman? What profession does this person have? How is this person dressed? What is the income level of this person — low, medium, or high? What is this person's pastime?

Now, look at that second doorway, and imagine that Ferrari — the brand — is standing there as a person. What kind of person would the Ferrari brand be? Is it a man or a woman? What profession does this person have? How is this person dressed — more formally or more casually than Mercedes Benz? What is the income level of this person — higher or lower? What is this person's pastime?

Now, compare the answers to both sets of questions. They're quite different, right? Even though Mercedes Benz and Ferrari are both high-end luxury cars that get you from one place to another, the brand images of Mercedes Benz and Ferrari are not the same. But why is that? It's because you *perceive, think,* and *feel* differently about these two brands. Your perceptions, thoughts, and feelings have been carefully created in your mind by smart marketers who understand the art and science of branding.

That's right. Branding, whether of a product or a person, is both an art *and* a science. On the one hand, brands appeal to your logic — they're rational in terms of how you think about them. This is where the science comes in. But branding is also an art because brands appeal to your emotions in terms of how you feel about them.

Consider This

Think for a moment about the brands that have earned your loyalty. Maybe you've even traveled out of your way to find and buy that special brand that's like no other. What if you could harness that same kind of power in your own job search? How would *you* like to have that kind of influence over a recruiter or a potential boss?

Branding People?

I firmly believe that people — just like shampoo and other products — are brands, too. Let's use examples of people we probably all know — starting with celebrities. What do you perceive, think, and feel when you hear the name "Brad Pitt?" What do you perceive, think, and feel when you hear the name "Johnny Depp?" Both of these actors are good-looking leading men, but they create very different perceptions, thoughts, and feelings, don't they? Now, let's throw "Jackie Chan" into the picture … you have different perceptions, thoughts, and feelings about him, too, right?

Think of any category of well-known people — how about singers this time? Think about Britney Spears … Madonna … Celine Dion. Again, they're all very different. That's because each of these individuals has a very specific personal brand that is absolutely unique and ownable as compared to the others.

"But, wait a minute," you may be saying. "Those people are all celebrities, and they have the money and the means to hire full-time image specialists to manage their personal brands!"

Fair point! But you don't need that kind of high-priced help to define and communicate your job-seeker personal brand. The personal branding system shared in *How YOU™ are like Shampoo for Job Seekers* will help you build your personal brand without writing checks to a publicist. It's designed for the millions of job seekers all around the world who may not be famous and certainly don't plan on turning their personal brand into a global household name. What you want to do is define yourself in *your world* in order to achieve your ultimate personal career goal: to land the job of your dreams.

When it comes to job seeking, your personal brand is defined as:

> *The way you want potential employers to*
> *perceive, think, and feel about you*
> *as compared to other candidates.*

Just as name brands exist in our minds, your job-seeker personal brand exists in the minds of recruiters and potential employers in the way they perceive, think, and feel about you as compared to other candidates. Let's look carefully at this definition, and focus on three key words: perceive, think, and feel. They've been carefully chosen for a reason.

Perceive: Perception is reality in marketing. When it comes to your job-seeker personal brand, it doesn't matter who *you* think you are. What matters is how the *interviewer* perceives you. If your potential employer sees you as very different from who you actually believe you are inside, you're probably not communicating the personal brand you want. You'll want to do some work to make sure you're presenting your best job-seeker personal brand in interviews.

Think: On the one hand, our brains have a lot to do with how we *think* about brands, so branding is a fairly rational exercise. There are logical reasons we choose one brand over another. The same holds true when using personal branding for a job search — you need to consider what your potential employers will *think* about you. What are the logical reasons a potential boss would choose you over another candidate?

Feel: On the other hand, branding is also a very emotional process. Stop and think about that one brand you said you were intensely loyal to earlier in this chapter. What is the feeling you have about that brand? Trust? Reliability? We establish connections with name brands, and these connections go far beyond just what the products do for us. We are loyal to these brands based on emotional connections. It's the same in personal branding. The way potential employers *feel* about you has a profound influence on your success. The stronger the connections you create before, during, and after your job interviews, the more powerful your personal brand will be throughout your job search process.

Colleagues' Brands at Work

Still don't believe the average person has a brand? Think of someone from your current job or your most recent job who you really enjoy working with — the kind of person you look forward to seeing and speaking with every morning. Stop for a moment and consider: How do you perceive this person? How does this person make you feel? What do you think about this person?

Now, consider a different person you work with or have worked with in the past … and let's be honest … who you really *don't* enjoy all that much! It's that one person who seems to cause you problems and tie your stomach in knots every time you have to work with them. How does *this* person make you feel? What do you think about this person, and how do you perceive him or her?

Can you see how these people have very different personal brands? And their brands have nothing to do with who *they* think they are. Their brands exist in *your* mind, based on how you perceive, think, and feel about them. If they haven't taken the time to define their best possible personal brand, they may be seriously limiting their success by presenting themselves in a way that differs from how they want to be seen.

Taking Control of YOU™

Now apply this thinking to you and your job search. As I said earlier, you, too, already have a personal brand, even if you didn't think you needed or wanted one. Your job-seeking personal brand may be out there doing its thing, creating perceptions about YOU™ without you even being aware of it. Interviewers may be thinking and feeling about you in ways that aren't at all how you want to be perceived, just like Alfred Nobel. Most people I've met find this idea both intriguing … and a little bit scary. They don't like the idea that their personal brands may be running amuck — maybe even preventing them from getting the job they want — without knowing what to do about it.

How do you take control of YOU™ during the job search process if your job-seeker personal brand exists in the minds of your potential employers? What can you do to make sure your personal brand is what you want it to be in interviews and beyond? How do you want future employers to perceive, think and feel about you? What steps can you take to make your job-seeker personal brand something that is definable and that you own, and how can you communicate it effectively — before, during, and after a job interview?

These are the questions we will answer as you move through the steps of our job-seeker personal branding system. No matter how successful you feel you've been in your job search so far, once you carefully define your job-seeker personal brand and put it to work, you have the opportunity to truly distinguish yourself from other job applicants. And just like Starbucks can command a much higher price tag than a standard cup of coffee at a local café, so can YOU™ create a premium personal brand that commands a better position, higher starting salary, nicer perks, and ultimately, a more satisfying career.

Think of it this way: Your personal brand in the job search process is what you want to stand for in the minds of potential employers. Who is _____™? Insert your name in the blank, and let's begin.

"Personal Branding? You'll find that under
'Arts and Science'."

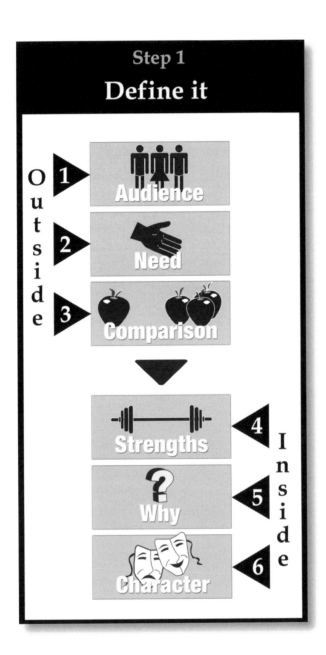

Step 1

Define it

Outside

1 Audience

2 Need

3 Comparison

4 Strengths

5 Why

6 Character

Inside

2

Defining Your Personal Brand

I always wanted to be somebody, but I should have been more specific.

— Lily Tomlin, Actress and comedian

Now you know you can't touch your personal brand because it exists in the minds of others. So, if you can't touch your brand, how can you master it in a way that actually helps you get the job of your dreams? It may seem like an incredibly tough challenge, but name brands have been successfully created in the minds of millions of consumers for years and years. You can absolutely take control of your job-seeker personal brand, too. Just like marketing experts have helped consumers choose one brand over another, you can use the same strategies to help potential employers choose you over the next candidate. The key is to do what all successful name brands do as a first step: *Define it.*

Fact: Every name brand you know and love uses six positioning elements to carefully define that brand. It doesn't even matter if the branders managing those brands are *aware* of these elements. Trust me — all six are a vital part of what makes the brand tick, and it's a tried-and-true formula.

You've already asked yourself the question, "Who is _____ ™ — the trademarked YOU™? And you may be saying, "But Brenda, I have no idea how to answer that question!" If this is the case, don't worry. We are going to work with a specific formula that borrows from the six positioning elements used by marketing experts around the world. That formula will help you pinpoint the best possible job-seeker personal brand for you — a personal brand that will present your best talents, strengths, and attributes and that helps distinguish you from other people applying for the kind of jobs you want most.

The Power of a Framework

Let's take a look at the six elements of this formula as they apply to the name brands we all love and use every day. Then, you will see how to apply those same elements to each one of us — as individuals — to define our unique personal brands.

THE SIX-ELEMENT FORMULA	
Name Brands	**Personal Brands for Job Seekers**
Target: When it comes to name brand products, this is the Target Market. Who will buy the product — men, women, college graduates, people with high incomes or low incomes? What are their hopes, dreams, and fears? What attitudes do they have toward the brand or the type of product in question? What can you tell about them by the way they act toward a particular brand?	*Audience:* Like a Target Market, your job-seeker Audience consists of the people you want to influence with your personal brand as you look for a job. Maybe your Audience is an individual, like a potential boss, or a group of people, like a division of a company. Who do you want to influence with your personal brand?

Need: What does the Target Market need? When a company creates a brand, they try to respond to a Need of ours that hasn't been filled yet. Or maybe they aim at meeting a Need we already have in a way that's better than competing brands.	*Need:* If your Audience is a potential employer, what does he or she need? Is there a gap that hasn't been filled in the company? For example, it's possible your future boss needs someone to take some responsibility off his or her shoulders.
Competitive Framework: When it comes to name brands, competitive framework is all about the brands that compete for your attention. You have many brands vying for your attention — why do you choose one brand over another?	*Comparison:* In personal branding, this is more about *comparing* than competing. Who will your Audience compare you to when it comes to meeting a Need you've identified? What other kinds of work experience might cause someone to be chosen for the job you want? What do you have to offer that will set you apart from other candidates?
Benefits: What does a brand offer its customers? Your toothpaste brand, for example, can help prevent your children from getting cavities, making you feel like you're a great parent.	*Unique Strengths:* In personal branding, your Unique Strengths are the promises that you bring to the table. Just like with name brands, your job-seeker Strengths are the *benefits* you can offer to a potential employer.

Reasons Why: Why should the Target Market believe a name brand can deliver what it says it can? These are a brand's Reasons Why. They can be based on a number of brand aspects, like its ingredients, its experience in the marketplace, how the product is designed, or maybe a strong endorsement.	*Reasons Why:* Why should a future boss believe you can deliver the Unique Strengths you promise? This is where you prove you can do what you say you can.
Brand Character: Think of this as the personality of a brand. What words would you use to describe a name brand if that brand were a person?	*Brand Character:* What is the Character of your personal brand? Think of this as a reflection of your personality, your overriding attitude, and your temperament. It's an important foundation of who YOU™ are.

Your Job-Seeker Personal Brand Positioning Statement

Hopefully, by now, you've asked yourself: "Who really is [insert your name here]™?" If you're not sure how to answer that question yet, don't worry. We're going to walk through each of these elements together in detail in the chapters that follow.

As we work our way through Step 1 — the "Define it" step — you'll be given the tools to complete a form called your "Job-Seeker Personal Brand Positioning Statement," which is set up in a format using the six elements from Step 1 of our system. Your Job-Seeker Personal Brand Positioning Statement will show you exactly how to define who YOU™ really are — which will help you to get the absolute best job for you.

Bottom line: This is where "you" become "YOU™."

As we work our way through each of the next six chapters, you'll be able to complete one more portion of your Job-Seeker Positioning Statement, just like the one outlined here. The second half of the book will show you how to communicate your well-defined personal brand before, during, and after job interviews. Then, you'll also learn how to avoid damaging the job-seeker personal brand you've worked hard to create.

YOUR Job-Seeker
Personal Brand Positioning Statement

Audience

My Audience is:

Company Facts:

Company Culture:

Division/Department Culture:

Interviewer:

Potential Boss/Supervisor:

Needs

Functional:

Emotional:

Comparison

Job Title:

Desired Identity: I want to be the brand of (*the way I would like to be perceived*):

Unique Strengths

My Existing Unique Strengths are:

The Future Unique Strengths That I Want to Work on Are:

Reasons Why

My Existing Reasons Why (*why my Audience should believe I can deliver my Unique Strengths*) *are:*

The Future Reasons Why That I Want to Work on Are:

Brand Character

My Personal Brand Character (how I want my Personal Brand Character to be perceived, including my overriding attitude, temperament, and personality) **is:**

By the time you have finished working with the six elements that define your personal brand and pulled together your Job-Seeker Personal Brand Positioning Statement, you'll be ready to put YOU™ into action. Armed with that, you will be able to demonstrate to your ideal employers exactly what you can do. Roll up your sleeves! Your personal brand is waiting…

Define it

Outside

1 ▶ Audience

Step 1

3

Audience

Job-Seeker Personal Brand
Positioning Element #1

It's up to the Audience. It always has been.

— Kate Smith, Singer

If you're unemployed or in a job that you don't like, let's face it: It's hard not to focus on yourself. All you want is to be gainfully employed with a steady paycheck and fulfilled by productive work. But the surprising truth about using personal branding in your job search is this:

**The best way to land the job you want the most
is to focus on your Audience.**

After all, potential employers (your Audience) are interested in what you can do for *them*. How are you going to make their jobs easier? What advantages are you going to bring to their company? Showing them what you can offer the company is how you get the job.

One of the most widespread myths about personal branding is that "personal branding is all about you." But think about it: If your brand exists in the minds of your Audience, how can it be all about you? It can't, and it isn't. So, the more you learn about your Audience, the more connected you will feel to the interviewer, the more you'll anticipate the needs of the company, and the faster you'll get the great job you really want.

How do you do that? Well, the key is to get as much information about the company as possible. In fact, one of the recruiters I interviewed said: "You want to stick out in an interview? Be knowledgeable about the company. You wouldn't believe how many people know virtually nothing about the company they're interviewing with. It's a big mistake."

If you learn about your Audience, you will have a head start on the interview process because you will already know more about the company than the majority of interviewees. A top pet peeve of many an interviewer is the applicant who doesn't do enough research prior to the interview. For example, one of the human resources pros I spoke with said: "It isn't enough in an interview to simply say, 'You have an opening in my field, and I know this is a good company.' But you'd be surprised how many people do exactly that." As you can imagine, that isn't enough. You need to have a very specific reason for wanting a *particular* position at a *particular* company. And the only way you can determine if a company is right for you is to learn about that company. Then, you will be prepared to tell your interviewer that reason.

Your interviewers will remember you if you can give them a detailed reason why you want to work there, if you've taken the time to read about the company's background, and if you've learned about the company's recent dealings.

Who is Your Audience?

So, how do you go about getting that information in order to connect with your interviewer? Let's assume you're a top-notch marketer. You are the newly-promoted Brand Manager of YOU™. You're in charge, and it's your job to see that your brand reaches the top.

If YOU™ were a product, your Audience would be called the "Target Market," and you would find out all you could about your target through surveys and questionnaires aimed at finding out who they really are. You would want to know provable facts about the people in your Target Market, like their age, sex, income, education, etc. How much do they earn? Do most of them live in the city or in the suburbs? In marketing, these provable facts are called "demographics." That's the kind of information you would start with.

An average marketer might stop there, but provable facts are only the tip of the iceberg when it comes to learning about the Target Market. Think about it for a moment: If you really want to get to know someone, is it enough only to know his or her age, how much that person earns, or where he or she was born and lives? It wouldn't really tell you much about that person, would it? You would only have scratched the surface, and you would need to base all of your assumptions about that person on little more than what you could read in a census form.

That's why top-notch marketers take the time to go deeper. They want to know much more about their Target Market. They want to get into the heads of the people who are buying their brands and understand their behavior. In marketing, this information is called "psychographics," which sounds pretty heavy, but basically means personal information that tells you what makes a person tick.

How does this apply to personal branding? Well, in general, your Audience is anyone or any company you want to influence with your personal brand. In your job search process, this includes the people who could hire you for the great new position you'd love to have. Your Audience might simply be the person who interviews you, but you may not know at first who your interviewer will be or even your potential immediate supervisor. So, in the beginning of your job search, your job-seeker personal brand Audience might be the entire company or a group of people within the company, such as the division or department where you'd like to work.

Now, you're probably thinking: "But how can I know so much about an Audience that I haven't even met yet? I don't know anyone at most of the companies where I will be applying for a job. In fact, to be perfectly honest, I don't even know which *companies* I'm interested in yet!"

Yes, it's true that when you're looking for a new job, learning about your Audience may seem challenging at first, and even choosing companies to target can be confusing. But learning about your Audience before you land the job is definitely doable, and all it takes is some smart investigating, which can actually be fun if you let it. With a little bit of sleuthing, you can find out which companies are the best fit for YOU™. In fact, you may be surprised how much you can learn about a company and its people with just a little bit of ingenuity and effort.

Getting Ready to Get Ready

When you're at the very beginning of your job search, you're in more of a *company* search than anything else. There are literally thousands of companies out there, so choosing the right ones to target may feel like looking for a needle in a haystack. But as the determined Brand Manager of YOU™, it's your task to decide which companies should receive your resume — the ones that will truly turn into an Audience for your job-seeker personal brand.

How do you do that? Start by asking yourself some questions about the "type" of companies you would be interested in. What is most important to you?

- Location?
- Size of the company?
- Culture of the company?
- Learning and training opportunities?
- Opportunities for advancement?
- Whether the company gives back to the community?

You might even rate these elements from 1 to 6 — with 1 as your highest priority and 6 as your lowest priority. Once you've decided what aspects of a company matter most to you, it will be easier to dive deeper and find out more about the companies that fit the bill. You'll then learn what you need to know to determine if a company is truly a good fit for you.

If you don't know which companies in your field are out there, do an Internet search and begin to gather names. Then, you can look through their websites and see how they measure up on your rating scale. As you begin to see which companies have the qualities and opportunities you're looking for, you can narrow down your choices.

Become a Creative Detective

Once you've selected your top companies, it will be time to get out your detective's magnifying glass. At this point, the Audience for your job-seeker personal brand is the entire company you're targeting. Of course, that doesn't mean you're expected to learn about every single person in a big company. Not only is that impossible, but it's not even necessary to get the job you want.

Instead, you can think of the entire company as an "individual" with its own set of facts and attitudes. As a great marketing sleuth, you can take what you learn about a company and begin to piece together a profile of how it operates, just as you would if you were learning about one particular person. You'll discover if the company has a relaxed, more casual atmosphere or a more structured, buttoned-down way of functioning.You will find out if the company finds innovation important or if it values adhering strictly to policy— that type of thing. Here are some of the ways you can dig deeper to find out more about your companies of interest:

Talk, Talk, Talk. Take the time to ask your friends and other people you meet if they know anyone who currently works for, or formerly worked for, your target companies — your potential Audience. If the employee is someone your contact knows well, you could even call or e-mail that person to ask them a few questions about the company.

Meet and Greet. If you get an opportunity to attend an event where you'd have the chance to meet people who work at one of the companies you've targeted — by all means, take it! Of course, in that kind of situation, it's important to keep up a professional image — even if it's a casual event — because you'll be meeting people face-to-face for the first time.

Search the Internet. Thanks to the worldwide web, it's easier than ever to find out a lot about potential employers. The number of online directories has quadrupled in the past ten years. While reviewing the company's website is the absolute best first place to start, it still only scratches the surface of what you can discover about a company online. With just a few research skills, you can mine an enormous amount of great information that you can use to put together a more detailed profile of your target companies.

Try typing the following into your search engine to discover more about a company:

[Company name] [your desired division or department]

[Company name] annual report

[Company name] press release

[Company name] event

[Company name] brochure

[Company name] newsletter

[Company name] e-zine

[Company name] charity

[Company name] values

[Company name] culture

Through these searches, you should be able to find out a great deal of information, including:

- How does the company present itself in the media?
- What is the tone and style of the various documents the company publishes?
- When you read the company's annual reports, brochures, newsletters, and e-zines, what facts and attitudes do these documents reveal about the company?

You'll be amazed at the amount of information you can gather about potential employers this way. What other aspects of a company are you interested in? Use your search engine, and see what comes up.

The Old Stand-Bys. You can look up companies on a number of traditional lists such as Standard & Poor's, Dun & Bradstreet, Dow Jones, Moody's Investors Service, and Polk's. While not all countries will be represented, many international companies are included. If searching these lists online requires that you pay a fee, check your local library to see if you can use the printed versions of these publications there for free.

Information from these lists and the company's website can help you uncover the following:

- Is the company on the stock exchange, or is it private? Family-owned?
- Does the company do business locally or internationally?
- How long has the company been in business? Has it changed owners more than once?
- What other companies are its biggest competitors?
- Has the company grown in recent years, or is its industry suffering?
- What trends taking place in the world today might have an impact on the company's business?

Articles About the Company. Search for articles about the company on the Internet, too. You will no doubt find dozens of online articles, or even hundreds if it's a large company. If you find references to printed publications with articles, go to your library to look them up. There, you'll find answers to questions such as:

- Has the company been in the news lately? If so, why? What are others saying and writing about the company?

- Where does the company as a whole place its focus?

- Has it merged or set up partnerships with any other companies?

- Has it introduced new products or services?

- Has it hired new executives?

- What charities has the company supported, and what do these charities say about the company's character and values?

- Is the company actively involved with the charity or simply making contributions?

- What is the primary focus of the charities — humanitarian, environmental, local, international, educational, or other?

Articles By or Regarding Key People. Try another Internet search for articles by or about some of the company's top executives. These will give you a good feeling for the company and what it's all about. You may even find articles that reference a key individual before he or she joined the company. If this person could be your immediate boss or the head of your potential division, knowing this background will tell you a lot about the kind of people the company values. You might even be able to find direct quotes from some executives to give you an inside look into facts about this person and what kind of behaviors they like or dislike. No matter whether this person is likely to be your interviewer or not, by understanding more about a company's execs, you will develop a more in-depth profile of the company and its important players.

Articles will also give you a good idea of the kind of experience the company is looking for. If you can find out the background of some of a company's current employees, you might start to see patterns in the types of people the company likes to hire. This kind of probing is definitely worth your time. If you look long and hard enough, you might even find an article mentioning someone who holds or who held the very same position you want!

The LinkedIn Advantage

Social networking sites like LinkedIn.com are another great source of company information. You may even discover companies of interest that you didn't know about. For example, LinkedIn hosts hundreds of interest groups, and if you search for groups in your areas of interest, you should be able to find others in your targeted industry who are working for great companies.

You can search for specific companies, a city you're interested in, or a particular industry. Make sure to search for old friends and classmates as well to find out where they're working. You might end up with a direct connection at a great company that you didn't even realize you had!

When you search for one of your targeted companies on LinkedIn, you'll find lists of those companies' employees who maintain LinkedIn profiles. Look for people working in the division you're interested in, for example, and read their information. You will find out more than you ever thought possible. These profiles often even include testimonials, so you can get a sense of the kind of people the company tends to hire.

When you review the profiles, look for trends rather than just specifics about individuals. Does a particular company's employees have things in common that could help you create a company profile? For example:

- Are the profiles similar in tone — such as all very buttoned-down or all quite casual?
- In what age group do the people listed tend to fall?
- How many years of experience or what level of education do most of the employees mention in their profiles?
- What is most often mentioned in the testimonials of the company's employees? Do they tend to focus more on creative input … loyalty … integrity?

When you have a list of the company's employees who have LinkedIn profiles, you will probably be amazed to discover how connected we all truly are to one another. Remember that old Kevin Bacon game that showed how everyone in Hollywood was only six degrees separated from him? LinkedIn works off that same idea — that everyone is only six degrees away from linking with everyone else. In other words, if you set up a profile on LinkedIn and invite others you know into your network, you will begin to create more and more connections. LinkedIn can search your address book in Microsoft Outlook or your e-mail list from many different servers and tell you automatically who on your list already has a profile on the site. You may even find out that you already know someone at one of your targeted companies! But even if you don't, you may still be able to establish a connection with someone.

Here's how it works. Let's say someone in your network knows someone in one of your targeted companies, and you see the number "2" by the employee's name on LinkedIn. This means that the employee you want to meet is only one connection away from you — someone in your own network knows that person directly. LinkedIn then allows you to ask that friend in your network to introduce you to the employee by sending an e-mail to that employee through the LinkedIn system — and you're off to the races!

If you see a "3" next to the name of the person you want to meet, it means you're two connections away from that person. So, you would need to request two introductions in order to meet him or her. That means you could ask the friend in your network to set up an introduction with the other person connected to the employee. Then, hopefully, that person would be willing to set up an introduction for you directly with the employee in question. That's a fair amount of work, of course, so you'd want to make sure that the connection will really be beneficial to you.

If you're only one connection away from an important company employee (a "2"), it should be easy enough to get an introduction, and it's well worth the effort. So, don't be shy about making these connections. If someone is unwilling to help you out with information about the company, that's fine, but you may also meet a great ally who could even help you get a job that's better than you had hoped for.

Culture is Key

As you sift through all of the information on LinkedIn (and elsewhere), see what it tells you about the company's "culture." Every company has a culture, and it's usually driven by its top leaders. So, reading LinkedIn profiles of a company's top executives can be really helpful, too, giving you a good sense of the company's values based on how its leaders are presented.

As an applicant, fitting in with the company's culture is key. First of all, if you don't fit in, you'll have a harder time getting a job. Second, if there isn't a cultural "fit" once you do get the job, you'll probably be unhappy there.

Is Your Audience's Culture Right for YOU™?

Gary Woollacott, CEO of Opus Recruitment, tells the story of a woman named Angela who was invited through his firm to interview with a bank. Despite Gary and Angela's high hopes, the interviewer didn't like Angela all that much. That very same day, however, Angela interviewed at a competitive bank and was hired right away. Angela was equally qualified for the first job as for the second, so what happened?

It turns out that the first bank was very structured, and Angela thrived in an environment where someone gave her the baton and let her run with it. The second bank was a good fit because it was looking for someone who could take charge and move forward independently, while the first bank wanted someone to follow specific protocol. One was clearly right for Angela, and one was not.

So do your research on the "culture" of your target companies. The more you know about the company's culture, the better you'll be able to tell if it's a good fit for YOU™.

The Right Questions

What questions should you ask someone who works at one of your targeted companies when you have the chance to speak with them? The best suggestion: Simply ask for advice! Be honest, and let that person know you're interested in working for the company. Ask them what they would recommend as first steps. You may be surprised by how much someone is willing to help you just because you've asked that one simple question.

Here are a few other questions to ask if you get the chance to talk to someone who is already part of an organization you're interested in:

- What key characteristics does the company look for in an employee?

- What do you think are the top five skills the company values most?

- What do you like the most about working there? What do you like the least?

- What's the length of the typical work day?

- Is it a training-focused company? If so, does it send employees to outside training programs, or does it hold regular in-house trainings?

- What are three words that best describe the culture of the company?

- How does the company treat its employees in general?

- Does the company hold a lot of events for its employees? If so, what kind?

- On a scale from 1-10, how open to new ideas is the company? Can you share some examples of why you would give it that score?

- Would you say that the company is more team-oriented or individual-centric? Can you share with me a few examples of why you think that?

The answers will give you great clues as to what to emphasize in your resume and interview. If you find out the company values integrity and collaboration skills, you can prepare examples to share in an interview about situations from the past where you've shown integrity and collaborated well.

Of course (and this does happen), in the process of collecting answers to your questions, you may find out you no longer want to apply to a particular company. This is a good thing! Scratch that company off of your list, and focus your well-honed energies toward a job in a different company that's a better fit for your talents and priorities.

Once you know about your target companies, you can use the same ideas to find out about the division or department where you want to work. Most of the time, there's a wealth of information out there about the particular area you're interested in.

The Inside Scoop from HR Professionals

Your initial cover letter will make more of an impact if you mention something specific about the company that you've learned through your research. Of course, don't simply say, "I read that the company appointed a new Chairman of the Board." Most people will know that! You need to make the item you mention relevant in some way, such as: "I was impressed to read Acme doubled its revenues in the past fiscal year," or "As an animal lover, I was very excited to read about Acme's involvement with the Wildlife Conservation Society."

Don't do what one candidate did and bring up in his cover letter the story he'd read about the company's legal woes. That might help you stick out ... but not in a good way!

Find Out About the Interviewer

Sometimes, you may be told who your interviewer will be, and sometimes not. If you're only given a title, simply ask for the person's name. Otherwise, you can do an Internet search for the company name and the interviewer's title to see if a name shows up. No matter how you manage to get the name of your interviewer — which is a bit of a golden key — type the name into a search engine like Google.com. Also, look for him or her on LinkedIn.com, Facebook.com, Myspace.com, and other social networking sites. Knowledge is power! So, the more you know, the better prepared you will be for the interview. You may not want to mention any of the information you have discovered in your search, especially if it's something personal like the name of the interviewer's children, but the information you find may tell you a fair amount about the interviewer's personality.

The more information you can find out about your interviewer — within reason, of course — the more confidence and understanding you will bring to your interviews.

What Type of Interviewer Will You Have?

If possible, try to find out if you will be interviewed by a human resources professional or a line manager. Why? Human resources managers sometimes focus more on the items on your resume than on whether you would be a good fit for the company. They may feel more at risk in the hiring process and want to make sure they do a good job of screening candidates. As such, they may stick to the basics and spend more time asking questions about the experience required for the job.

Line managers, on the other hand, are considered to be a bit more lenient when interviewing candidates for their division. That's because they are the ones who know best how well a person would fit into a particular job and within the specific culture of the company or division. A line manager is more likely to evaluate a candidate's overall presentation rather than specific skills, experience, or education.

Your Job-Seeker Personal Brand Positioning Statement

You're now ready to begin completing your Job-Seeker Personal Brand Positioning Statement.

To help you with your own statement, let's look at some examples. I have included the Job-Seeker Personal Brand Positioning Statements of two people who have different backgrounds and job search objectives. As we work through the chapters, we'll follow along and see how these two people have completed each section of their own Job-Seeker Personal Brand Positioning Statements. These examples will hopefully give you lots of ideas and will help you understand how your own Positioning Statement all fits together into a cohesive whole. We'll even show you how our two job seekers went about their own Audience research and what methods they used to find out about their main target company. Let's start with Jamie.

Case Study – Jamie Nelson

For three years, Jamie worked on the multimedia team at Axion, a high-tech company that began struggling about a year after he was hired. When the company was bought out by another firm, Jamie was laid off. Axion was Jamie's first job out of college, and he had hoped to build a career there. So, at 25 years of age, Jamie was frustrated to find himself on the job market again. But once he began to investigate companies and target his search more carefully, he started to feel more excited about the possibilities. He decided to try and use this job change as an opportunity to get an entry-level position in management. He had dabbled in management at Axion but never held a manager title; nonetheless, Jamie felt he was up for the challenge.

A search of the Internet for "DVD design expansion" and "DVD design services" led Jamie to an article and a press release about a company that was expanding its DVD department into the 3D area. He felt it would be a good fit for him because of the company's plans for expansion and because Jamie had solid education and experience in this area.

Jamie's Job-Seeker
Personal Brand Positioning Statement

Audience

My Audience is: PreLife, a multimedia firm that is expanding into 3D DVD design.

Company Facts: PreLife is a company with about 150 employees located a 25-minute drive from where I live. The company was founded in 1999 and has grown fairly rapidly. The DVD department is one of the fastest growing areas of the company, and the focus on 3D design is just now starting.

While PreLife hadn't yet placed an ad for any jobs related to the new 3D department, one of Jamie's connections on LinkedIn.com gave him an introduction to someone who works in a related department. That person was able to offer Jamie some helpful information about the company's culture. Jamie found press releases about recent hires and looked those employees up on LinkedIn.com and Facebook.com, too. As a result, he found out the following information about the company:

> **Company Culture:** PreLife is all about innovation and creativity. They have a track record of hiring younger employees because the company finds fresh new ideas just as important as experience. The company has no problem hiring a manager in his or her 20's as long as the person in question demonstrates management potential.

Jamie's new contact at the company was able to give him some inside information about the company's culture and about some of the challenges PreLife was facing.

> **Department Culture:** The DVD department is interested in managers who can take the reins of projects and run with them, making sure no existing clients are lost during the new staff's learning curve. The culture is also very much a team atmosphere, where everyone's input is valued. PreLife makes it a point to hire people who are creative, so everyone has the potential to contribute. But the company has grown so fast that a lot of new employees need to be trained; for example, they're behind in getting everyone up to speed on the new 3D DVD design process and how the new area of focus will run effectively.

Based on the information Jamie found, he sent an unsolicited cover letter and resume to PreLife and was excited to get a call a week later from HR, asking him to come in and interview for the new position of Assistant Manager of the 3D DVD department. While on the phone, he asked who he'd be interviewing with and found out that he'd be meeting with his potential boss — the Manager of the new 3D DVD department, Tom Brunnell. Jamie typed Tom's name into Google.com and also looked Tom up on LinkedIn.com.

Interviewer: I will be interviewing with Tom Brunnell, the 30-year old manager of the new 3D DVD department. He has been with the company for four years. From Tom's LinkedIn.com profile, I can see he is very well liked because he has recommendations from some of the employees he manages. Tom calls himself a "computer geek" in his profile and says that he just can't get enough of technical knowledge. This is something I have in common with him. He graduated from Georgia Institute of Technology and spent four years working for a small (now defunct) digital media company, first as a team member, then as an Assistant Manager.

Case Study – Marcia Jenkins

At 32 years of age, Marcia had been working as an Accounting Manager for a large multinational corporation in the fast-moving consumer goods industry. Her goal was to be promoted to Accounting Director, but she had already been passed over twice for the director job. Given her company's "up or out" policy—where you either keep moving up or you have to move on—she felt the writing was on the wall: Clearly, she would eventually have to find a new position outside the company. While she enjoyed the culture of her current employer, she didn't feel her contributions were valued enough. She was frustrated and wanted to find a company that would truly appreciate what she had to offer. Marcia felt she was ready for an Accounting Director position—one that would excite and challenge her.

Marcia had already had one interview with her target Audience, another large multinational that manufactured a wide range of food products and had divisions on three continents. The corporation was healthy, its stock price was doing well, and she discovered through speaking to colleagues that the company offered its employees more perks than her current firm. While attending a charity cocktail party, Marcia found out about an opening as Accounting Director in the Snacks Division at this target company. Marcia had to follow up twice with the HR department after submitting her resume, but she finally got an interview. In her first interview, she met with a representative from Human Resources, and that meeting went well. Marcia created this Job-Seeker Personal Brand Positioning Statement as she was preparing for her second interview with Bina Tilak, the Vice President of Finance for the Snacks Division.

Marcia's Job-Seeker
Personal Brand Positioning Statement

Audience

My Audience is: Samson Foods International

Company Facts: Currently, this company has almost 17,000 employees across multiple offices in North America, Europe, and Asia. The company has dozens of well-known brands and is growing. In fact, to make room for this growth, the company recently expanded its offices to an additional floor in its headquarters here, and it's opening two new offices overseas right now as well. The Snacks Division is among the fastest growing divisions of the company, and that's where the company is looking to add talent.

During her first interview, Marcia liked the fact that everyone she saw in the office was dressed in professional business attire. Just like her current employer, the atmosphere was fairly "buttoned-down," which was just what Marcia liked. Employees appeared really motivated and driven — working hard — as they walked through the office when Marcia was there for her first interview.

Company Culture: I was told in my first interview that the corporation values loyalty and looks for people who want to commit long-term. They believe in offering their employees the same kind of loyalty, which includes a fair number of incentives and assistance, such as training opportunities, chances for advancement, an onsite cafeteria at discounted prices, annual bonuses, and two holiday parties — one for the adults and one for children of employees. It's a buttoned-down atmosphere, with everyone dressed very professionally and sticking to fairly strict but unwritten "look" guidelines.

The HR rep that Marcia met in her first interview was up front with Marcia about the fact that, about a year ago, the corporation had actually promoted someone from within the company to the position of Accounting Director – Snacks Division. However, that person hadn't worked out as the company had hoped. So, they began looking outside the company to fill the position. During this same first interview, Marcia found out from the HR rep that Bina Tilak is "known for her attention to detail and desire to be kept up-to-date on a regular basis as to what's going on in the Division." Marcia got a strong sense that the former Accounting Director who had been promoted from within failed to keep Bina up-to-date on what was happening.

Interviewer: Bina Tilak was promoted to Vice President of Finance about one year ago after five years of holding the position I'm applying for. In the press release about Bina's promotion, I read into it that Bina is a no-nonsense go-getter who expects a lot of her staff because she expects a lot of herself. From my first interview with the company, I found out that Bina is a bit of a perfectionist, and I get a sense she has a tendency to micro-manage her direct reports. From what the HR rep told me, I think Bina may have some "trust" issues since it appears that the former Accounting Director made some poor decisions without consulting Bina that negatively impacted the division.

Now, you're ready to complete the Audience portion of your own Job-Seeker Personal Brand Positioning Statement. If you have more than one target company, you will want to do separate Audience definitions for each target.

YOUR Job-Seeker
Personal Brand Positioning Statement

Audience

My Audience is:

Company Facts:

Company Culture:

Division/Department Culture:

Interviewer:

Potential Boss/Supervisor:

> *The best way to land the job*
> *you want the most*
> *is to focus on your Audience.*

Define it

Outside

2 ▶ Need

Step 1

4

Need

Job-Seeker Personal Brand Positioning Element #2

Before you build a better mousetrap, it helps to know if there are any mice out there.

> — Yogi Berra, Professional baseball player and manager

It isn't enough just to know who your Audience is. You also have to know what your Audience *needs*. Good marketers won't build a better mousetrap unless they know there are people out there with a mouse problem who need that mousetrap. If the marketplace doesn't need it, they'll end up with a warehouse full of mousetraps and no one to buy them.

It's the same with personal branding. You want to find the companies that need what you have to offer. Some people just cast a wide net and apply for jobs at all sorts of companies without any sense of direction. But if you try to get a job with a company that has no need of your talents and experience, you're actually slowing down your job search. The outcome? Nothing but frustration and disappointment. If you spend the extra time and energy to really do your homework, you'll get a much better and faster result — a job you know is the best fit for you.

So, the next step in defining your personal brand is to take all of the information you've gathered about your Audience and determine what that Audience *needs*.

Fix the Problem

Needs are an important part of each and every name brand that exists out there. What do we mean by a Need? Well, there are three ways a good marketing team looks at Needs for a brand like Nike or Nestle:

- A problem that requires a solution,
- A problem that is not now being met well enough in the market, and/or
- A new problem we didn't even know existed.

For example, Pert Shampoo (called Wash & Go or Rejoice in some countries) was the first brand to come out with a shampoo and conditioner all in one bottle. What need did it fill? The need for speed and convenience in the morning in order to get out the door more quickly. When Apple discovered that consumers needed a more user-friendly computer, it developed the Mac. Viagra was the first drug to solve the problem of "erectile dysfunction."

What about a Need that is not now being met well enough in the market? This is an example of Yogi Berra's proverbial "better mousetrap." Gillette created a razor that gives you a better shave. Nokia went beyond just technical needs to market their phones as a fashion statement. And while Viagra tackled erectile dysfunction, Levitra did it one better when it proved it could provide erections for a full 24 hours. Cialis then filled yet another Need in the marketplace since it is able to provide erections for 36 hours, causing the drug to be dubbed "the weekender." How's *that* for a better mousetrap?

Then, there are the Needs we didn't even know we had. Who knew we needed to carry around tiny contraptions that would hold every song we could possibly ever want to hear? Apple did, so it created the iPod.

Likewise, when Howard Schultz visited several coffee bars in Italy, he noticed that they offered much more to their patrons than just coffee. They gave people a place to meet where they could sit for long periods of time and talk. Customers weren't being rushed out the door in order to let someone else have their table. They could relax and spend quality time together. Schultz saw a Need that most of the world didn't even know existed, and Starbucks was born.

Finding an Audience That Can Use Your Talents

Rebecca had just celebrated the purchase of her first house when — wham! — her finance company downsized and got rid of a lot of employees, including Rebecca. She was suddenly in the job market again and terrified she wouldn't be able to find a job where she could earn enough money to pay her new mortgage every month. She had ten years of experience supporting technology systems in financial services firms, but there just weren't a lot of openings in her area with established companies.

Rebecca sat and thought about it ... and then, a light bulb went off in her head. She came to realize that with her good experience, she could train entry-level new hires that needed development in technology. When she shifted her thinking from providing services to in-house clients to providing *training* on the same type of technology to new hires, she found a consulting company that needed exactly that. She now loves her new job teaching and sharing her skills with new team members. It has opened up a whole new world to her — and she's happy in her new home (and making regular mortgage payments, too).

The lesson here is to make sure you stretch your thinking. What Needs in the marketplace can you already meet based on your work experience? Don't limit your thinking only to what you have done so far. What else can you bring to the table? When you discover a company's Need, ask yourself if you could possibly meet that Need — whether or not you've done it before.

Function and Emotion

In the name-brand world, the Needs of a Target Market can be either functional or emotional. What are some examples of functional Needs? Crest toothpaste fills the functional Need of fighting cavities. Gatorade fills the Need of quenching your thirst. Both of these examples are *physical*. But a functional Need can also be something non-physical yet still tangible, like the Need for a smaller, lighter-weight digital camera.

On the other hand, emotional Needs — as you might suspect — have to do with feelings. Because Crest protects your child's teeth from cavities, it also fills an emotional Need of making you feel like a good parent. Your Allianz AG homeowner's insurance policy gives you peace of mind because you know you can replace all of the things you own if you're robbed. Get the idea?

So, which type of Need is most important — functional or emotional? The answer is: *both!* The best brands are designed to hit both of those types of Needs smack on the head. That powerful combination is what builds the most successful brands. Here are some examples:

♦ Bubble Wrap

Functional Need: *Protects your fragile items during shipment.*

Emotional Need: *Gives you 100% assurance that your cousin Mary's wedding vase will arrive at the church in one piece — not ten.*

♦ Viagra

Functional Need: *Um ... you already know this one, right?*

Emotional Need: *Puts the skip back in a man's step because his loving relationship is once again on track.*

♦ Starbucks

Functional Need: *Gives you a better tasting cup of coffee.*

Emotional Need: *Gives you a place where you can take a break during the day, have a tasty reward on a comfy couch, and meet your friends for a leisurely visit.*

The allure of Starbucks' emotional need is strong. Think about it: If Starbucks had stopped at only meeting its Audience's functional Need of a better tasting cup of coffee, it might never have achieved such huge success. After all, there are lots of great cups of coffee out there, right?

So, just as these name brands make sure they fill both the functional and emotional Needs of their Target Markets, it's your job as the Brand Manager of YOU™ to make sure you meet both the functional and emotional Needs of your Audience as a key part of your job search. But how exactly does this tried-and-true branding concept apply to YOU™? And how can you use it to hone in on — and land — a great new job?

Functional Needs for Job Seekers

First, like any good Brand Manager, you'll want to figure out your Audience's functional Needs. In personal branding, functional Needs are typically described as the roles you play — the services you could provide in your new job. Think of it as a combination of the tasks listed in the job description along with the job title: tax accountant, human resources manager, operations specialist, finance director, etc. In other words, when thinking of functional Needs, ask yourself what you would be hired to do. If you're an office manager, you'd probably take care of your Audience's Need for efficient office operations, keeping the office machines running, hiring new team members, keeping the supply cabinet full, etc.

Functional Needs are also related to your knowledge, experience, and expertise. If you're hired as a graphic designer, it's automatically expected that you're going to be creative. If your job title is Public Relations Director, it just goes without saying that you will have a full address book with dozens of great connections in your field.

Emotional Needs for Job Seekers

But how do you apply *emotional* Needs to the job-seeking YOU™? Let's look at name brands again. When you're loyal to a particular brand year after year, you've gone beyond just the functional or physical Needs that brand fills for you. You have entered "Brand Land" — the place where a brand has created a true emotional connection with you. A while back, a participant in one of my Personal Branding workshops admitted she was so dedicated to her L'Oreal skin cream that she said, "They'll have to pry it from my cold, stiff fingers once I'm gone." Now, *that's* a strong emotional brand connection!

Take me as another example: I've been using the same brand of toothpaste every single day for over 30 years now. *Thirty years!* But I've only been married to my husband for ten years ... so, statistically, you might say I'm more likely to cheat on my husband than to switch toothpaste brands! (Of course, I wouldn't do that, but I do admit to being very loyal to my brand of toothpaste.) The point is: Some people would rather trade their spouse than switch to a different brand of cereal. When you make that kind of emotional connection with your Audience, you've created true brand loyalty.

Okay, so you aren't a brand of cereal, but that's exactly why it's easier for your Audience — your targeted potential employers — to forge an emotional connection with YOU™. Have you ever had the experience where someone in your company or someone from a nearby department kept coming back to you, asking you to do more work for them? This is no doubt because you met that person's emotional Need by building a relationship of credibility and trust. The functional Need you met was the work you actually did, but more than that, this person knew you would deliver quality work on time again and again. Just like with my favorite toothpaste, *that's* powerful branding.

What Do Your Potential Employers Need?

How do you determine the functional and emotional Needs of the companies you've targeted in your job search? First, to sniff out functional Needs, check out job descriptions on Internet job sites, in newspaper classified sections, or on the company's website. Most job descriptions contain only a portion of what's actually required for the job, but they can give you a good general overview of what the company is looking for, particularly from a functional standpoint.

If a recruiter is involved, you should be able to find out more details from him or her about the company's Needs. Maybe a friend of yours knows an employee in the company, or maybe you can connect with a current employee through LinkedIn. If that's the case, try to get the inside scoop on what the position requires. Here are some questions you can ask about the job:

- How do you see the responsibilities of this position?
- What qualifications and qualities are required do to this job well?
- What kind of person is the company looking for to fill the position?
- Who last held the position, and why did that person leave the job?
- Why was that person either a good or not so good fit for the job?

One thing to watch out for, though: Recruiters caution against asking too many inside questions of people you don't know well. One recruiter told me: "Even if your intention is good, it's easy to come across as a snoop. But if a trusted friend of yours knows an employee of the company you're interested in, send an e-mail or make a quick call to let that person know you're sincerely interested in learning more about the job that's available. Then, ask some general questions about the position."

Play Analyst

When you get your hands on a job description, take off your Brand Manager hat for a minute, and put on your Analyst hat. Size up the job description for both functional and emotional Needs. Let's take a look at this example from a recent job posting:

Merchandise Manager for Fine Handbag Company

Major Responsibilities Include:

- Develop, implement, and maintain product assortments that support planned sales strategies.
- Manage inventory levels to maximize profitability and achieve financial objectives.
- Develop and recommend promotional plans.
- Serve as primary store and vendor contact.
- Collaborate with internal departments to support company-wide initiatives.

Position Requirements:

- 5 years or more experience in related buying and planning position.
- Supervisory experience.
- Strong merchandising, product, and mathematics skills.
- Proficiency with these software programs: Word/Excel/PowerPoint.

Ideal candidate will have two or more years experience with a handbag design manufacturing firm, as well as proven leadership skills and the ability to make key decisions with regard to product line discontinuations.

Based on this description, the functional Needs of the company are obvious, which is a good thing! You know the company's functional Needs include about five years of experience and the ability to perform the major responsibilities. But what about the emotional Needs of this job? The company uses the words "develop" and "manage" in the description, which means they need someone who can take charge and see a project through from beginning to end. They need an individual who is capable of working independently and getting things done. When I sit back and look at that, "reliability" comes to mind as an emotional Need for this company.

Keeping that in mind, if you were to interview for this job, you would want to share specific stories and examples of how your former employers could count on you to get the job done. You might mention, for example, the details of an experience where you managed a project to successful completion. One human resources executive I interviewed told me: "Past tangible experiences that a candidate can relate back to my company mean more to me than anything on a resume."

"Supervisory experience" is also mentioned in this sample job description, so that tells me this employer needs leadership skills and that this job requires a sense of responsibility. If your potential boss knows that you can accomplish the job without hand-holding, he or she can then get on with running the business. That's how you fill an emotional Need.

What Needs Can You Fill?

When you're wearing your Analyst hat and reading through a job description, be sure to compare it with the job descriptions of your prior jobs. What responsibilities have you had in previous jobs that you could apply very clearly to this new company? What tasks are you able to perform that make you qualified for this position? Even more importantly, is there anything you can offer the company that is above and beyond the job description?

Another good hint: Look for a description of the "ideal candidate." In our example, it gives you a lot of ideas about what could give you the edge over other applicants. The more you're able to fill the shoes of the "ideal" candidate, the better chance you'll have of getting the job. What if you don't exactly fit the profile of the "ideal"? If you have most of the requirements for the job, don't let very specific qualifications stop you from applying for a job you really want. It may be that the ideal candidate never shows up for an interview, or the interviewer may have a better feeling about you and your personal brand than someone who looks ideal on paper. If you have "most but not all" qualifications they are looking for, don't hesitate — go for it! What do you have to lose?

You can also learn about the company's emotional Needs from the other kinds of "detective research" we talked about in the Audience chapter. These approaches will help you understand a lot about a company's values and culture, which are strong clues about the company's emotional Needs. Let's say you've discovered through your digging that your target company is a brokerage firm that prides itself on being honest and ethical, always following government rules to the nth degree. Perfect! Now, you can offer examples from your work experience that show how you overcame ethical dilemmas.

Below is a list of possible emotional Needs that your Audience may have. What other emotional Needs could you add to the list?

Trust	Honesty	Sincerity
Resourcefulness	Empathy	Encouragement
Creativity	Self-reliance	Diligence
Dynamism	Responsibility	Assertiveness
Reliability	Energy	Sense of Humor
Flexibility	Enterprise	Dedication
Objectivity	Tenacity	Thoroughness
Optimism	Patience	Conscientiousness
Imagination	Versatility	Determination
Tolerance	Intensity	Cooperation
Eagerness	Persuasiveness	Decisiveness
Loyalty	Dependability	Commitment

Once you have a full list, think about which of these Needs you think each target company most requires from you. Based on what you've found out about each company, make your most intelligent guesses. Then, narrow your list down to the top two or three that you believe will best fill the Needs of each company.

Now, ask yourself: What past experiences could I share with a job interviewer that would show how I can fill these most critical emotional Needs? This is key! And it's one of the best ways that you can begin to build an emotional connection with your interviewer. When you actually show the interviewer what you can do to make life easier for your potential employer — even in the short time span of a job interview — you are definitely pulling on emotional cords and building a strong job-seeker personal brand.

Your Job Search Personal Brand Positioning Statement

So, what does *your* Audience Need? Let's check in with our two fellow job seekers to see how they completed the Needs section of their Job-Seeker Personal Brand Positioning Statements. You'll see that they've identified the main functional and emotional Needs of the key company they're targeting. Use their statements to help you complete the Needs section of your own Job-Seeker Positioning Statement.

Jamie knows that creativity and innovation are important to PreLife, but he also knows that he needs to offer the company even more in order to stand out from other applicants. So, he plans to focus on the following based on what he's learned about what PreLife needs:

Jamie's Job-Seeker Personal Brand Positioning Statement

Needs

Functional: An independent-thinking 3D DVD development team leader who can stimulate his team to deliver innovative ideas that satisfy the customer's desired specifications while meeting or beating project deadlines.

Someone experienced enough in 3D DVD design to train staff members who are relatively new to this type of design.

Emotional: Someone Tom can count on to successfully implement new design ideas without a lot of hand-holding or supervision.

Marcia's Job-Seeker
Personal Brand Positioning Statement

Needs

Functional: A self-directed Accounting Director with the experience to delve right into the job with minimal training in the corporation's procedures.

A great communicator who will keep the VP of Finance up-to-date at all times as to what's going on.

Emotional: Reliability — Someone Bina can finally rely upon to take charge of the job quickly and seamlessly so that she can truly attend to her position as Vice President.

Trust — Someone Bina can be assured has good judgment and will know when to involve her when big decisions need to be made.

What are *your* Audience's Needs for your own Job-Seeker Personal Brand Positioning Statement?

YOUR Job-Seeker
Personal Brand Positioning Statement

Needs

Functional:

Emotional:

Define it

O
u
t
s
i
d
e

3 ▶

Comparison

Step 1

5

Comparison

Job-Seeker Personal Brand Positioning Element #3

Even if one is interested only in one's own society, which is one's prerogative, one can understand that society much better by comparing it with others.

— Peter L. Berger, Philosopher

Now that you have defined the Audience and Needs for your job-seeker personal brand, you're ready to move on to Comparison — the third key element that defines what your brand is all about.

Remember what we said about personal branding for job hunters? It's the way you want potential employers to perceive, think, and feel about you "as compared to other candidates." The Comparison element is where the "as compared to other candidates" part comes into play.

For marketers who manage big name brands, this element is called the "Competitive Framework." That's because name brands *compete* with one another for a share of the profits in the marketplace. There are only so many buyers of shampoo in the world, for example, so Pantene and Sunsilk will each command a certain share of the "shampoo pie." (How's that for a tasty-sounding treat?) The makers of each brand will always look for new ways to drive their share up and take a larger piece of the pie from other brands.

But in personal branding, there is no "market share," so this is where personal brands and name brand products are fundamentally different. I guess you might say this is one of those times when YOU™ *aren't* like shampoo!

When You're *Not* Like Shampoo

As a personal brand, if you have a piece of the pie, it doesn't mean you've taken someone else's portion, even if you're the one chosen for a specific job and they're not. That's because as humans, we are simply more multi-dimensional than name brands. Every one of us is unique. You are an individual, and it's up to you to determine your own specific personal brand and what role it will play in your career and in the workplace.

To show you what I mean, let's think again about celebrities. Yes, it's possible that Brad Pitt and Johnny Depp could compete for the same part in a film, but each of them would bring something entirely different to a specific role, wouldn't they? You can see why personal branding is not so much about competition as it is about Comparison.

Yet, your job-seeker personal brand exists in relation to other candidates, so no matter what you do, Comparison *is* an inherent part of how you define it. So, how do you succeed at the Comparison game?

Playing the Comparison Game

Here's a truth about interviewing that you may not know: It's often not the best qualified candidate who gets the job; it's usually the candidate who can best fill the Audience's emotional Need. For example, if two tax accountants are equally as good at filling the functional Need, your Audience is likely to choose the one who fills the emotional Need best. That might be the accountant who, during an interview, is able to relay stories from his or her past experiences that demonstrate reliability. Or it might be the one who presents the best "can-do" personality when meeting with the interviewer. This is the kind of Comparison that can win you the job you want.

Wear an Interviewer's Shoes

If you're trying to decide if it makes sense to apply for a particular job, try walking a mile in the interviewer's shoes. Again, it's about the Audience and their Needs, right? We all have room for improvement, so be honest with yourself. How would an interviewer see you as compared to other candidates?

- Have you been out of work for a long time?
- Have you held numerous jobs in just a few years?
- Were you fired from your last job for "less than desirable" reasons?

I'm not emphasizing negatives here — not at all, I promise — but a great Brand Manager needs to know the honest truth about what's great and what can be improved upon when it comes to the brand they're marketing. The same is true of personal branding. If you don't know what to improve, you really can't move up in the world. So, make a realistic list of how an interviewer might perceive you and your experiences as compared to others — and, yes, be sure to include both the good *and* the bad!

Once you have a better sense of how your interviewer might perceive you and your past work experience, you have a golden opportunity to counter your interviewer's fears by pointing out your more positive attributes. If you've made mistakes, be honest about them. But, even more importantly, immediately share with the interviewer what you learned from those mistakes and explain how you will be a better employee as a result. Doing so will not only show your character, but it will demonstrate that you're someone interested in learning, growing, and constantly improving throughout your career.

Plus, you already have the edge simply because you've put in the time and energy to learn as much as you can about the company. As we mentioned before, recruiters and interviewers complain time and time again that the majority of people who arrive for an interview know very little about the company. They get lazy. Don't let that be YOU™! Powerful personal brand builders stay the course and do the same amount of interview preparation for every opportunity. This alone will help you to stand out.

Now, what else can you do to give yourself a "comparative" edge?

Your Job Search Comparison

If I asked you, "What is Heineken?" you'd answer, "It's a beer," right? When it comes to name brands, the "average" marketer thinks of their brands that way. For example:

- Nikon is a … camera.

- Listerine is a … mouthwash.

- Harley-Davidson is a … motorcycle.

So, in personal branding, it would be easy to fall into the trap of seeing yourself as only the job title or the job description. Are you looking for a job as a:

- Human Resources Executive?

- Sales Representative?

- Media Coordinator?

- Chief Financial Officer?

Those titles don't tell you very much, do they? And they definitely don't tell you much about who you might be compared with for a job. It's just the tip of the iceberg.

When YOU™ Are More Than You

What could be more boring than a personal brand of "Sales Representative"? That label doesn't make you stand out from any other Sales Representative applicant, does it? That's why you need to create what I call a Desired Identity. Your Desired Identity will allow you to go beyond just that standard ol' job title. It's all about getting creative in how you think of yourself and how you could be compared with other candidates applying for the same job.

Great brand managers do this with the brands they manage. If Heineken only positioned itself as "a beer," it probably wouldn't sell very well. If Nikon was a manufacturer of just any camera, why would anyone choose it over another brand?

Richard Czerniawski and Mike Maloney, marketing colleagues of mine and partners in the firm Brand Development Network International, label this process the "Perceptual Competitive Framework" of a brand. Here are some well-known name brand examples of Perceptual Competitive Framework that Mike and Richard like to talk about:

Starbucks isn't just a coffee restaurant … it's a *rewarding coffee experience.*

Gatorade isn't just a thirst quencher … it's *the ultimate liquid athletic equipment.*

Snickers isn't just a candy bar … it's a *between-meal hunger satisfier.*

Nokia isn't just a cell phone … it's *fashion technology.*

McDonald's isn't just a fast food restaurant … it's a *fun family food destination.*

Let's look at this another way and stretch our minds a little bit using an exercise called:

When is an apple not just an apple?

If you looked at an apple as only an apple, then you would automatically think of it as a fruit, right? In this case, that apple would be compared to other fruits like grapes, bananas, or oranges.

But what if you looked at an apple as "a portable, ready-to-eat snack?" (And it is, of course!) If you did that, the apple could then be compared to other snack foods like cookies, granola bars, and potato chips.

Now, let's think of an apple as "a daily health maintenance provider." (Once again, it is that, too.) If you thought of an apple in that way, it could then be compared to vitamin supplements, exercise, and getting plenty of sleep.

But wait! You could also think of an apple as "a beautiful table-top decoration." (Yep, it is!) Then, you could also compare it to candles and flowers. Get the idea?

If you can get your Audience to think about YOU™ in that same expanded way, you can potentially fill all sorts of Needs you hadn't even thought about yet. And that's what can help you land the job you're dreaming of, even if someone else appears to have better credentials and experience. How's *that* for a "comparative" edge?

Never Get Typecast

If you're stuck in the rut of being typecast as an "Administrative Assistant," for example, it's time to expand the roles you can play. Think about how you want to be perceived, and let your imagination go. How can you change the perception of YOU™ from simply, say, a store manager to the "Take-Charge Guru"? If an interviewer thought of you that way, and a "take-charge attitude" was critical to the success of the job you wanted, you would almost certainly get that job. The "Take-Charge Guru" would become the Desired Identity of your job-seeker personal brand.

Below are some other examples of potential Desired Identities that you might want to communicate as part of your job search. How do you make sure you communicate your Desired Identity? The key is to offer stories during your interviews from your past job experiences that clearly show how you were the "Dynamo" or the "Innovator." You wouldn't necessarily refer to these titles in an interview, of course. (You don't want to come across as someone with super-hero delusions!) But it definitely helps to think of yourself this way. It gives you a focus for your job-seeker personal brand that's fun, and it's a great way to really stand out and get excited about what you can offer a potential employer.

By the way, if you're a natural storyteller, this part will come easily to you. If you're not necessarily a good storyteller, work on how to tell your stories ahead of time. Try them out on a friend or colleague before you actually get into an interview situation.

What examples can you share which would demonstrate that you are:

The "Get It Done Guy or Gal" — When your division was up against a challenge, people turned to you as the "closer." You were the person they relied on to finish the job. Offer a specific example from your past experience. Maybe you took charge of a problem project and found a solution that meant the project could be completed on time and within budget.

The "Connector" — You're always networking and know the perfect person for every task. Everyone at your previous job knew to "just give you five minutes to check your contact list," and they would instantly have a valuable person to call. Offer a story that shows how your vast connections benefitted your past employer. Maybe your company's printer couldn't do a job at the last minute, so you pulled out your mobile phone and called your old college roommate in the printing business, saving the day just in time.

The "Tension Breaker" — Your co-workers always counted on you when the tension was high to tell a joke and bring a smile to everyone's face again. Now, it's important to note that if you tell stories about breaking the tension, make sure you show exactly how it helped the work environment. You don't want to give the impression that you're someone who cracks jokes all day and gets nothing done. But a well-placed story about that time in your former job where you found a way to bring humor to a situation when everyone was tense, maybe even preventing an argument, can go a long way in the eyes of an interviewer.

The "Innovator" — When a new idea was needed, everyone knew to come to you for your imagination and creativity. This Desired Identity is easy to convey in an interview. Be ready to share several new ideas that you came up with and how they were successfully put into practice. If possible (and if it doesn't breach confidentiality), take actual figures with you to the interview to show how your great ideas increased your former employer's bottom line. That's powerful!

The "Dynamo" — When energy and tenacity were called for, you were the first person who came to mind at your prior company. You kept everyone motivated and on target until the job was done. While this might be a bit harder to show in an interview, share situations where you helped your co-workers to keep their eyes on the task at hand and got the job done despite obstacles.

"Mr. or Ms. Precise" — When something had to be done right the first time down to the last detail, everyone knew your work would be meticulous and exacting. Pinpoint and be ready to share examples of when co-workers or employers came to you for your precision. If you can quantify the results from this, arrive at your interview armed with the numbers. Was there a time when the accuracy of a report was vitally important to your former company, and your boss came to you because of his/her confidence in your strong focus on details?

These are just a few possible Desired Identities. What other Desired Identities can you come up with that highlight your specific talents?

Have Fun With Your Brand!

Nancy had been working as a Senior Administrator, but when her company merged with another, her seniority dropped dramatically. She realized it would take a long time for her to move up in the newly formed company. Nancy had worked on her personal brand before, while on the job, and she had chosen a Desired Identity of "The Swiss Army Knife of the Executive Suite." She liked this Desired Identity a lot, so she decided to keep it for her Job-Seeker Personal Brand Positioning Statement as well.

When Nancy went out on interviews, she actually decided to tell her potential employers that she was known at her company as the "Swiss Army Knife of the Executive Suite" — the person who's ready and willing to take on whatever responsibilities are needed and use her creativity and resourcefulness to get things done. She told a couple of stories from her job when she stepped in and made sure everything got done.

Nancy's Desired Identity was so distinctive and powerful that it made her memorable with interviewers. It also showed potential employers that she was willing to work hard and make a significant contribution to any company. Within a very short time, she was able to find a better job with a higher salary in part because her Desired Identity gave her a unique personal brand that was much more exciting than just "Senior Administrator."

The moral of this story? Whether or not you think it makes sense to actually tell your interviewers your Desired Identity, enjoy the opportunity to be creative as you come up with ways YOU™ can be more than just you. That's how you succeed at the Comparison game.

There's More to YOU™ Than Meets the Eye

Smart job seekers will come up with a Desired Identity that will help them in their job hunt, so it's time to be imaginative and look beyond the obvious. What more can YOU™ be? Brainstorm until you come up with many possibilities, and let your mind run wild without censoring.

You never know when a gem may come out of something that at first seems pretty crazy.

Try to think of several possible Desired Identities that a potential employer might find powerful based on what you've learned about the companies you are targeting for jobs. Don't feel you have to think of all of the possibilities in one sitting. You can always come back with fresh eyes at a later time to find new ideas, some of which may just pop into your head during the next few days. And don't hesitate to ask friends and colleagues to brainstorm with you.

Example: I'm not just a Senior Administrator; I'm the Swiss Army Knife of the Executive Suite.

Now, you try it:

I'm not just a _____; I'm a _____.

How many Desired Identities can you think of?

Who Do YOU™ Most Want to Be?

Now that you have exercised your imagination, how do you decide which Desired Identity you will apply to your job-seeker personal brand — the brand that will help land you that dream job? One way to choose is to go back to the Needs section of your Job-Seeker Personal Brand Positioning Statement. Ask yourself which one of your potential Desired Identities will best fill your Audience's Needs. And, most importantly, which Desired Identity is most in line with who YOU™ really are and with your real career passions?

Remember: When you make your choices, they don't have to be engraved in stone. As you work through the elements of your Job-Seeker Personal Brand Positioning Statement, you may find that you have two or three Desired Identities you could communicate effectively. You might even want to use one Desired Identity for one specific target company and another for a different company. If so, that's perfectly fine. For now, make choices based on the companies where you'd most like to work. This will help you to move forward in the process of creating your Positioning Statement.

Your Job-Seeker Personal Brand Positioning Statement

So, how did Jamie and Marcia apply these ideas to their statements? Take a look below.

Jamie's Job-Seeker Personal Brand Positioning Statement

Comparison

Job Title: Assistant Manager – 3D DVD Department

Desired Identity: I *want* to be the brand of *(the way I would like to be perceived)*: **"Finish Line Champion"** — A reliable Assistant Manager who takes the reins at the starting line and motivates the team through the race, getting the project to the finish line in record time.

Marcia's Job-Seeker Personal Brand Positioning Statement

Comparison

Job Title: Accounting Director – Snacks Division

Desired Identity: I *want* to be the brand of *(the way I would like to be perceived)*: **"Experienced, Trusted Communicator"** who uses good judgment to make sure work is done efficiently and accurately and who always communicates fully with the VP of Finance.

Now, you're ready to take what you've learned and apply it to your own Job-Seeker Personal Brand Positioning Statement. I hope this chapter brings new creative spark to your job search and helps you see how you can definitely win at the Comparison game — and have fun doing it.

YOUR Job-Seeker
Personal Brand Positioning Statement

Comparison

Job Title:

Desired Identity: I *want* to be the brand of *(the way I would like to be perceived):*

> « *If two candidates are equally as good at*
> *filling the functional Need,*
> *your Audience is likely to choose the one*
> *who fills the emotional Need best.* »

Define it

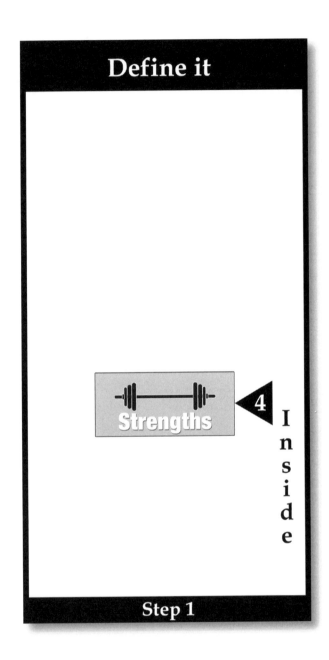

Strengths

4

Inside

Step 1

6

Unique Strengths

Job-Seeker Personal Brand Positioning Element #4

*Every person born into this world represents something new,
something that never existed before, something original and
unique. It is the duty of every person ... to know and consider
... that there has never been anyone like him ..., for if there had
been someone like him, there would have been no need for him
to be in the world.*

— Martin Buber, 20th century philosopher
and author

If someone who knows you and your work well was stopped in the middle of the street and asked — "What does _____ [insert your name here] stand for?" — what would this person say about you? What would they share that is specific to who you are and what you can do? These are your Unique Strengths. They are the nuts and bolts of your job-seeker personal brand — where the rubber hits the road when it comes to branding yourself.

In the world of name brands, Unique Strengths are called the "Benefits" that a brand offers — the most meaningful promise that a brand can, and wants to, own in the mind of its Target Market. Let's take a recognizable brand as an example. When you hear the name Volvo, what comes to mind? Safety, right? This is the Benefit that sets Volvo apart from Mercedes Benz, Chrysler, Toyota, and every other car brand on the market. Volvo has done such a great job with its brand image that I suspect it's perceived by most people all around the world as the safest brand of automobiles available.

How does this apply to personal branding? Well, for a name brand, the Benefits answer the Target Market's question: "What's in it for me?" For personal branding during a job hunt, your Unique Strengths answer your Audience's question: "What's in it for the company?" They tell your potential employer what you can offer their organization if you're hired.

Consider This

When I speak or conduct a training about personal branding, an audience member will inevitably approach me and say, "The truth is, Brenda, I'm not really that unique. I don't think what I have to offer is very distinctive. My contributions aren't any different from anybody else's." And, often, no matter how hard I try, nothing I can say seems to change their minds.

But recently, I bought a new Toshiba laptop computer that helps bring home the point of how unique each one of us truly is. You see, my new computer comes with a very nifty feature — "biosensor fingerprint identification." That means the computer has software that records and recognizes my fingerprint. It then uses my fingerprint as the "password" for accessing my keyboard, hard drive, bookmarked log-in pages, etc. No other fingerprint will do! It has to be my right index finger and mine alone.

I'm totally enamored with this new "toy" of mine. But besides that, I'm also excited by this constant reminder that each one of us is so incredibly unique. Every time I start my computer with my unique fingerprint, I think to myself: "No one else on the face of the planet can do that." I'm the only individual out of the 6 billion+ people who call this earth home who can simply "swish" a finger over the top of that biosensor and unlock this computer. My husband has tried, my assistant has tried, my family members have tried … but, nope — it's my fingerprint, or it just won't work. How powerful is that?

Okay, so you already know that you have a different physical makeup from everybody else. But it makes sense that if your fingerprints and DNA are so unique, then so is the exact configuration of your talents and attributes. It's an absolute impossibility that anyone else can contribute to a company in exactly the same way as you. So, recognizing what you truly have to offer and learning to leverage that during your job search is what your job-seeker personal brand is all about.

It's a matter of defining clearly what makes you truly distinctive (beyond your fingerprints). That's the key to successfully branding yourself. Your very individual combination of values, passions, and talents is what unlocks the real YOU™ — just like my fingerprint unlocks my computer. It's up to you to discover and celebrate your uniqueness. Then, you will know exactly what you can offer to a new company that no one else can.

Unearthing Your Strengths

So, how do you figure out what your Unique Strengths are? There are many ways you can nail them down. Allow yourself some good quality time to think about what you have to offer, and try these ideas to begin uncovering the Unique Strengths you already have:

Pay Attention. Simply listen to what people say when they talk about you. When you're introduced to someone, what words are used to describe you? How do your friends introduce you to someone new? Have you ever given a presentation or received an award? If so, what Unique Strengths were highlighted when you were introduced? If you haven't been formally introduced anywhere recently, do you have any programs or materials from past events that would contain a description of you written by someone else?

Performance Reviews. If you're like most people, you focus on your weaknesses when reading your current and past performance evaluations. But if you take a second look at reviews you've had on the job, you will most likely see Unique Strengths that are consistent throughout. What do the comments say about your specific talents? Read between the lines to learn what qualities truly differentiate you from others. If you don't have any personnel reviews from your former jobs, think about the jobs where you thrived. When your supervisors or co-workers complimented you, what did they say? What types of work did you do best, and what types of jobs did you like the most?

Take Personality Profiles and Tests. There are several personality tests that can give you insight into your Unique Strengths like Myers-Briggs (www.myersbriggs.org). You may unearth several new things about yourself in the process of taking these tests. If you purchase the book, *Now, Discover Your Strengths*, you can access the computerized quiz at www.StrengthsFinder.com, which will uncover your top five Strengths.

There are lots of personality tests out there, and we've checked out a few for you. Look for our recommended list in Appendix B at the back of the book, and try them out.

List Your Values. Take stock of what values are most important to you. If being trustworthy is key, for example, this may be a Unique Strength you want to apply to your job-seeker personal brand. If loyalty is most important to you, maybe that's the Strength you most want associated with your name. Your list of values will help you to determine which of your Strengths hold the most meaning for you. If you care deeply about the Unique Strengths that are a fundamental part of your job-seeker personal brand, you'll be even more passionate about what you do.

As you create your list, however, make sure you don't borrow someone else's values. Sometimes, the values of your peers or parents can get mixed up with your own, but you need to make sure the foundation of your personal brand is authentically yours.

List Your Passions. People often do best at the activities they love to do the most, so your Unique Strengths are directly related to what excites you. If you're passionate about your Unique Strengths, that passion will move you forward and help you do well, and you'll enjoy every minute of it. Yet, we often become so involved in the "shoulds" of life that we forget about our passions.

My passion is brands. I love them, I study them, I know them, and I teach them. When people who know me hear the name "Brenda Bence," they think "branding." So, make a list of the activities and things that make you feel enthusiastic and joyful, and don't limit the list to activities that are only related to business or work. You may find something unexpected among the passions in your life.

Ask Your Friends and Colleagues. You can't uncover your Unique Strengths only by searching within. Ask your friends and co-workers to tell you what they think are your Unique Strengths. Ask them to tell you what they believe is exceptional, rare, and special about you. Be sure to ask these questions of people who know you well, and let them know you want honest answers from them.

Asking for feedback can be uncomfortable, but without it, you will end up with a very narrow view of your Strengths. Nine times out of ten, others judge you less harshly than you judge yourself, and they will notice positive aspects of YOU™ that you may have overlooked entirely. So, don't be afraid to ask for feedback — it's a key way to discover the perfect Unique Strengths for your job-seeker personal brand. Only then can you be sure that you won't undersell or oversell yourself in the job search process.

Here are some questions you could ask others, but feel free to add to the list:

- When you think of me, what are the first positive traits that come to your mind?
- What special talents do you think I have?
- What attributes do I have that stand out from others?
- What, if anything, is exceptional or rare about me?
- What would you consider my very best qualities?
- What would you recommend to others about me or my work?
- If you were trying to convince someone to hire me, what would you say?

Now, make a list of your Unique Strengths. Have you discovered any that you didn't know you had?

Your Audience Needs YOU™

Here's a fundamental fact when it comes to branding whether it's for name brands or for personal branding:

Your Unique Strengths must respond to your Audience's Needs.

And, if you remember, Needs come in two forms — functional and emotional. So, in keeping with that, your Unique Strengths also need to be both functional and emotional.

Let's look at Volvo again. Safety is the functional Need that Volvo fills because Volvo's cars have been built to keep you from getting hurt in case you're in an accident. But driving a Volvo also gives you peace of mind, so the brand fills one of your important emotional Needs as well.

In personal branding, a functional Unique Strength might be something like your ability to provide reports that are very detailed. You might call this "accuracy." An emotional Unique Strength could be the fact that you provide those reports on time every time. You might call this one "reliability." Get the idea?

Your Functional Unique Strengths

First, let's consider the functional Needs of your Audience. Which of the Unique Strengths on your list will best address those Needs? Be honest and realistic about how well your Unique Strengths actually meet your Audience's Needs.

It's okay if you don't have a Strength to match every one of your Audience's Needs. This will tell you where you want to focus and develop new Unique Strengths to help strengthen your job-seeker personal brand. These will become what we'll call your "Future Unique Strengths," and we'll call the strengths you can already provide your "Existing Unique Strengths."

Here's a scale to help you rate how well your functional Unique Strengths actually meet your Audience's functional Needs. Go through each of your Audience's Needs and choose from 1 through 6:

1 = I can't respond to this Need at all.

2 = I can respond slightly to this Need but below average.

3 = I can respond to this Need at an average level.

4 = I can respond to this Need well.

5 = I can respond to this Need to a large degree.

6 = I am outstanding at responding to this Need.

Here's an example:

> **Functional Need of Your Audience:** Accurate Financial Reporting
> **Your Functional Unique Strength:** Precision
> **Your Rating from 1-6:** 5

Once you're done, sit back and look at what you've written. How did your functional Unique Strengths rate?

Your Emotional Unique Strengths

Now, let's consider your Audience's *emotional* Needs. Which of your Unique Strengths would best address the top emotional Needs of your Audience?

Rate how well your emotional Unique Strengths meet your Audience's emotional Needs using our scale:

> *1 = I can't respond to this Need at all.*
> *2 = I can respond slightly to this Need but below average.*
> *3 = I can respond to this Need at an average level.*
> *4 = I can respond to this Need well.*
> *5 = I can respond to this Need to a large degree.*
> *6 = I am outstanding at responding to this Need.*

Here's an example:

> **Emotional Need of Your Audience:** Turning financial reports in on time
>
> **Your Emotional Unique Strength:** Reliability
> **Your Rating from 1-6:** 4

If you find that your Strengths don't respond to your Audience's Needs as much as you'd like, don't worry! Remember that you will have both Existing and Future Unique Strengths, and your Future Unique Strengths will give you something to work on as you develop your job-seeker personal brand and work toward landing that great job.

How Did You Do?

Now that you've rated your Unique Strengths against your Audience's Needs, you will fall into one of four categories. Which one best describes you?

1. I already have the Unique Strengths that respond to my Audience's Needs, and I already communicate these Unique Strengths on my resume and during interviews.

2. I already have the Unique Strengths that respond to my Audience's Needs, but I'm not yet consistently communicating these Unique Strengths on my resume or during interviews.

3. I don't have the Unique Strengths that meet my Audience's Needs right now, but I'm going to work on developing them because it will help me get the job I really want.

4. I don't have the Unique Strengths that respond to my Audience's Needs and — if I'm honest with myself — I'm not willing to develop them because they would be too far away from who I really am.

If you fall into the first category, congratulations! Your Unique Strengths are ready to serve your job search well. All you have to do is continue to work on your Unique Strengths and make sure that you highlight them on your resume and in interviews, sharing real-life examples of how you've used those Strengths in previous jobs.

If you fall into the second category, your job now is to make sure your Unique Strengths come through loud and clear on your resume and in interviews. Don't worry — the next section of the book will show you many ways to do just that.

If you fall into the third category, you have discovered that your current Unique Strengths aren't quite enough for the job you'd really like to have. That's okay. You may have some work to do, but you can take charge and make a plan to develop the Unique Strengths you need for your best possible job-seeker personal brand. You have the willingness and the passion to do it, and you will, even if it means that you have to work your way up the ladder to reach that ultimate job.

If you fall into the fourth category, you may have discovered that you're headed in a direction that is — quite frankly — not likely to make you happy. It can be a bit discouraging to find yourself in this situation, but it's a great opportunity to do some helpful soul-searching. You may need to consider looking for a different type of job. You'll have a much better chance of getting a position where your Unique Strengths would be valued, and you'll enjoy a job much more if that position allows you to use your true talents. Either way, you now know that you should pursue a career that better matches your Unique Strengths, and you will no doubt be happier for it in the end.

Listening to Your Passions

Sharon had been working in sales in the telecom industry for almost nine years when a restructuring caused her position to be eliminated. It was incredibly stressful, and Sharon was totally exhausted from the experience. So, she decided to take a break to figure out what she wanted to do next. Her frustrations with the situation were so demoralizing that she soon decided the best next step would be to change industries entirely.

Since her specialty within the telecom industry was on the decline, she focused her new job search on a growing industry — health care — something that she had always been passionate about. Sharon went through dozens of interviews with a number of health care companies, but it didn't take long before she realized that she simply didn't have the industry knowledge to start in a job at her desired level. She would have to begin in a very entry-level position because her Unique Strengths just didn't fit the companies' Needs.

After months and months of interviewing, Sharon realized it was time to rethink her strategy. She considered the telecom industry again, but if she was honest with herself, there was only one telecom company that she would consider. The company was a global player and one that was much more influential than her previous company. Even though the idea of re-entering the telecom field seemed like a disappointment to Sharon, she decided to apply for a job with the global telecom player.

When she finally arrived for her interview, Sharon told me she felt "this incredible feeling of being *home*" as soon as she entered the building. She understood the lingo and the culture. It was a comfortable "fit" for her. She could even make sense of the jargon that was written on a white board in the conference room where she waited for the interviewer. She suddenly realized that this environment — this industry — was exactly right for her, and she felt she could excel again at what she knew best.

A light went off in Sharon's head, and in that split second, she was able to recognize the value of her prior training and experience. She said to herself, "I'm going to go for this," and she felt in the pit of her stomach that she would get the job. And she did! In fact, her new employers had even heard great things about her from other players in the industry, so she was a very desirable candidate in their eyes.

After running away from telecom and battling so hard to get into the health care industry, it took Sharon entering this company's offices for the interview — seemingly defeated — to show her that her real Unique Strengths lay in her knowledge and passion for telecom. She had let one bad situation turn her off from recognizing her true value. In the end, Sharon ended up finding just the right Audience and just the right place where she could best use her Unique Strengths.

The point is this: Even if you didn't like your last job, it doesn't mean that you wouldn't like another job in the same profession or industry. Think about where you will feel a sense of belonging and where you believe you can best contribute. That's where your Unique Strengths will be appreciated, and that's where you're likely to find the job you'll be most passionate about.

Streamlining Your Strengths

You've scored yourself against your Audience's Needs, you've uncovered your Unique Strengths, and you have a good long list of both. Now, it's time to make choices. You have to choose which of your Unique Strengths will be the truly critical Strengths you want to stand for — i.e., the heart of your job-seeker personal brand. Of course, keep in mind: The Unique Strengths you choose should also respond well to your Audience's Needs.

Choosing isn't always easy, but as Author Peter Drucker said, "Wherever you see a successful business, someone once made a courageous decision." The same holds true for personal branding.

Let's look at Volvo once again as an example. It's easy to remember that the brand stands for safety. If the brand tried to stand for safety plus reliability, beauty, innovative style, and unusual extras, you would lose track, wouldn't you? Most name brands try to own no more than one or two specific benefits. Pantene owns healthy and shiny hair. Head & Shoulders owns beautiful, dandruff-free hair. It isn't that these are the only benefits these brands offer. They may also have a nice fragrance, contain moisturizing ingredients, and help repair split ends, etc. But good marketers make choices, and that means sticking to just one or two Strengths that the brand truly wants to — and can — own.

So it is with personal branding. As the Brand Manager of YOU™, it's your job to choose two to three — four maximum — of your top Existing and Future Unique Strengths that you can, and want to, own.

Many people balk at this. They say, "Wait a minute, Brenda! I'm much more multi-dimensional than that. I have a lot of Unique Strengths, and I want to use them all in my job search as well as in my future job." And, of course, you should use all of them, and you will. Choosing now doesn't mean you won't work on additional Unique Strengths that you want to develop later on. But which are the Unique Strengths you want most to be associated with your job-seeker personal brand? You need your Audience to be able to remember what you stand for (whether or not they will ever verbalize it). Your Audience can only retain so much, and you really need to be focused and consistent in order to be known for your Unique Strengths and remembered by interviewers.

As you reflect on your Unique Strengths, think once again about how you would like potential employers to perceive, think, and feel about YOU™. What are the three or four key qualities that you want to pop into the minds of interviewers? Which Strengths are the most meaningful and will differentiate you the most? How would you like to be remembered after your next job interview? And do these particular Unique Strengths address your potential employer's greatest Needs?

As you're looking for that great new job, it may be that one of your target companies has different Needs than another. You might decide that you want to focus on one of your Unique Strengths with one company and another Unique Strength with a different company. This is absolutely fine if you think it's appropriate. But do try whenever possible to focus your job-seeker personal brand on the three or four Unique Strengths that differentiate you the most. That kind of consistency always pays off in the end.

Your Job-Seeker Personal Brand Positioning Statement

Spend some time with your list of Unique Strengths until you feel comfortable with (and excited about) the two or three most important ones. In the meantime, take a look at the Unique Strengths of Jamie and Marcia.

Jamie's Job-Seeker Personal Brand Positioning Statement

Unique Strengths

My Existing Unique Strengths are:

- Provider of new and innovative ideas in multimedia design that satisfy customers' needs and meet or beat project deadlines.
- Demonstrated ability to train others in DVD design.
- Strong history of self-management.

The Future Unique Strengths That I Want to Work on Are:

- Team leadership and management skills — ability to take a small group of people forward and make creative decisions, especially when there is little time for on-the-spot direction.

Marcia's Job-Seeker Personal Brand Positioning Statement

Unique Strengths

My Existing Unique Strengths are:

- Outstanding accounting experience and credentials.
- Strong self-management skills.
- Clear and regular communicator.
- Reliable and trusted decision-maker.

The Future Unique Strengths That I Want to Work on Are:

- Adjusting style to work well with a boss who is more of a micro-manager.

When you've narrowed down your Unique Strengths to those you want to apply to your job-seeker personal brand, add them to the Unique Strengths part of your Job-Seeker Personal Brand Positioning Statement, dividing them between Existing and Future Unique Strengths. This will tell you which strengths you can apply immediately to your personal brand and which ones you need to work on.

YOUR Job-Seeker
Personal Brand Positioning Statement

Unique Strengths

My Existing Unique Strengths are:

The Future Unique Strengths That I Want to Work on Are:

" *It's an absolute impossibility that anyone else can contribute to a company in exactly the same way as you.* "

"That picture portrays his desired
Unique Strengths!"

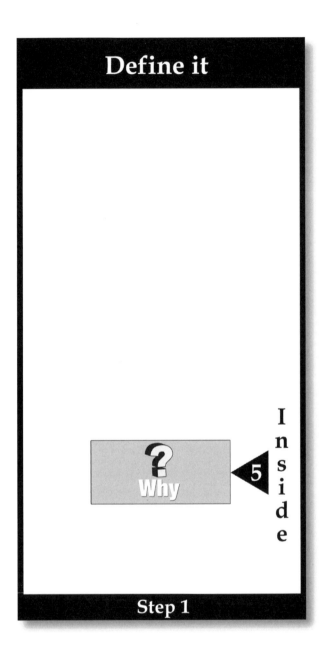

Define it

Step 1

7

Reasons Why

Job-Seeker Personal Brand Positioning Element #5

To be persuasive we must be believable; to be believable we must be credible...

> — Edward R. Murrow, U.S. broadcaster
> and journalist

You're getting close to finalizing the definition of your job-seeker personal brand! We're moving on to personal brand positioning element number five — your Reasons Why. This refers to the reasons why your Audience should believe you can deliver your specific Unique Strengths. It's all about credibility, and it's absolutely fundamental when it comes to looking for a new job. Your Reasons Why give potential bosses reasons to trust you can do what you claim you can do.

Returning to name brands again, they also have Reasons Why that can take on many different forms. Here is a list of some popular brands and the Reasons Why you and I believe those brands can deliver what they promise.

Brand	The Reason(s) Why	Type of Reason(s) Why
Dove	1/4 Moisturizing Cream	Ingredient
Neutrogena	#1 Dermatologist Recommended	Endorsement
Google	PigeonRank™ Search Technology	Design
Patek Philippe	Watches Are Handmade	Process
Heineken	Europe's #1 Imported Beer	Market Experience
Evian	Water from Source Cachat	Source

In *personal* branding — especially when it comes to using your personal brand to get your foot in the door of a new company — your Reasons Why mainly come in three forms:

Education. Maybe you have a degree from a reputable university or you attended a special training course that makes you uniquely able to deliver your Strengths. Or maybe you went to a seminar that gave you some great insight into your industry.

Experience. Your past work experience can be a powerful Reason Why. Perhaps you've spent many years in the field, or you've written an article on a topic related to one of your Unique Strengths. Or maybe you've given lectures, conducted a study, or been involved with a project that makes you particularly qualified to deliver your Unique Strengths.

Endorsements. Someone who knows you well may offer a reference that gives your Audience a good reason to believe you can do what you promise. In the hiring process, references — which are a form of endorsement — can be incredibly important. When someone with a good reputation speaks highly of you, it's a powerful Reason Why someone would choose to hire you as compared to someone else who is applying for the same position. One human resources professional that I interviewed said: "Never underestimate the power of a good testimonial or reference. What someone else has to say about you makes a big difference to potential employers."

Whatever the form of your Reasons Why, they need to be powerful enough to make your Audience believe you can deliver what you say you can in a way that uniquely responds to their Needs.

Your interviewer has no personal experience of you on the job, so you have to make your Reasons Why both dynamic and believable. Every time a company hires someone new, it's a bit of a risk, and the person doing the hiring is trying to reduce that risk as much as possible. So, it's your job as the Brand Manager of YOU™ to convince your potential employer that you can deliver your Unique Strengths. Without Reasons Why, it's almost impossible to do that. That's why Reasons Why are so critical.

The Reasons Behind Your Strengths

A Unique Strength without a Reason Why is like an airplane without wings — it will never hold up. Think about it: If a brand of shampoo simply said it was the best shampoo on the market, would you believe it? No, you'd want some form of proof that this shampoo is better than the rest. You'd feel better knowing it contains a new patented ingredient that adds luster to your hair or perhaps hearing it's been formulated with a specific vitamin known for keeping your hair healthy. So, it's very important that each one of your Unique Strengths also has a specific Reason Why in order to justify your Audience's trust in you.

How many reasons can you think of that would prove to your Audience that you can deliver each of your Unique Strengths? Think about them in terms of the three types we talked about earlier: education, experience, and endorsements. Which category or categories do your Reasons Why fall into?

Here's an example:

Unique Strength:

Creates innovative software programs

Reasons Why:

- *Experience:* Seven years experience in the field of software development.

- *Education:* A degree in computer technology from New York University including participation in the development of two award-winning software programs.

Review each of the Unique Strengths you chose from the last chapter, and write down your Reasons Why for each.

Then, sit back and look at your Reasons Why, and consider objectively whether they're truly strong enough or compelling enough to convince your Audience you can deliver your Unique Strengths.

If you think they're not strong enough to support your Unique Strengths, or if you want to boost your Unique Strengths and make them stronger, you may need to develop new Reasons Why. Just as we called your Unique Strengths either Existing or Future, we will also divide your Reasons Why into Existing and Future. For your Existing Unique Strengths, you probably already have Existing Reasons Why in the bag. If you have a Future Unique Strength, however, you'll almost surely need a Future Reason Why or two to make that Future Unique Strength believable.

Could Your Existing Reasons Why Be Even Better?

If you believe your Existing Reasons Why aren't enough to prove to potential employers that you can deliver both your Existing and Future Unique Strengths, what Future Reasons Why could you work toward? Think in terms of your education, experience, and endorsements. What can you do to create more or stronger credibility to support your Unique Strengths? How can you use your Reasons Why to help your interviewer believe you're the right person for the job?

Creating a Reason Why

Adam was a Customer Service Officer who oversaw a small team of 20 people for a company in Canada. He had been in this position for seven years, and he had come to the conclusion that he just wasn't going any further. He wasn't growing or learning anything new, and on top of that, the company was beginning to experience some financial problems. So, Adam decided it was time to look for a job elsewhere.

He found a company that peaked his interest, and after reading website bios, press releases, and articles, it was clear to Adam that the company expected members of their customer service management team to be very visible in the community through publishing articles or giving talks on superior customer service. Adam had never considered doing anything like that, and truthfully — he hated to write. But he didn't mind giving talks. So, he decided to offer to give a talk at both a non-profit organization's management team meeting, as well as at an informal meeting of customer service representatives, just to see how it would all go.

Both organizations were happy to have him speak, and it gave Adam a strong Reason Why for his Future Unique Strength of "spokesperson for great customer service."

Armed with this experience, Adam went in for an interview with his target company and shared what he had done. It was enough to impress the interviewer, and this important Reason Why helped Adam land the job he wanted.

The moral of this story is: If you don't already have the Reasons Why you need, create your own! Find a way to establish yourself as more of an expert in whatever you do. What types of activities would set you apart? You don't necessarily have to give speeches, write an article, or author a book. Perhaps you could take a course or gain certification to prove that you can truly deliver your Unique Strengths. Whatever it is, focus on making YOU™ and your Strengths even more credible with strong Reasons Why.

Are Your Reasons Why Too Far in the Future?

You may find that the Future Reasons Why you need will take a lot of time and effort to develop. If this is the case, don't get discouraged. You may simply need to seek a "stepping-stone position" — one that will work as a next step toward that ultimate dream job — while you work on developing a stronger arsenal of Reasons Why.

Here's an example: Monica's dream job was to be a Senior Editor at a major magazine, but she knew she didn't have the kind of experience she needed to land that coveted job … at least not yet. For one thing, she had gotten sick and had to drop out of journalism school one year before she was scheduled to graduate. Then, the magazine where she worked as an Editorial Assistant went bankrupt, and she was suddenly out of a job. It was a string of bad luck that left Monica feeling pretty discouraged on the career front.

She spent four months trying to find a job as a Senior Editor, but it was clear that she just didn't have enough Reasons Why to support her for that level of job. Monica knew that her true dream of becoming a Senior Editor was not going to happen any time soon unless she took the bull by the horns. So, despite the financial risks, Monica decided to take out a loan to finish her journalism degree. In the meantime, she created a profile on LinkedIn.com, found some of her old classmates on the site, and discovered that a few of them were working for magazines and newspapers. Based on those contacts, she was able to get enough freelance writing assignments to pay her bills and even landed a part-time job as a Fact Checker for a small but reputable magazine.

Once Monica received her journalism degree, she worked on her job-seeker personal brand and spent time learning all she could about the culture of her favorite magazines. She then began to apply to the magazines that most interested her and ended up getting a job as an Associate Editor at one of her top-listed desirable companies. Within three and a half years, Monica had moved up the ranks at the magazine and distinguished herself enough to be offered the job of Senior Editor.

The point of the story? Monica may not have been able to land her dream job as fast as she would have liked, but she worked hard to make sure she had strong enough Reasons Why, and — with a little patience — she was able to get her ultimate job within a relatively short period of time.

Narrowing It Down

How many Reasons Why should you have in your Job-Seeker Personal Brand Positioning Statement? The answer depends on how many your Audience will find meaningful. In other words, how many Reasons Why do you need to truly differentiate YOU™ from other candidates? Perhaps even more importantly, how many can your Audience honestly remember? It's better to keep your Reasons Why to a minimum. Focus on quality, not quantity. The Reasons Why won't matter much if your Audience can't remember them at the very moment they're considering choosing YOU™ over someone else for the job you want!

If you aren't certain which Reasons Why to focus on, think back again to what you learned about your Audience:

- What have you learned about the companies you're targeting that can offer you clues about the types of Reasons Why they would value most?

- Have the press releases you've read focused more on new hires' education, or have they emphasized more about those new hires' past work experience?

- Are the bios of employees on the company's website heavy with mentions of their publications and/or speaking engagements or other types of high-visibility activities?

Just a little bit of research can help you learn what each company considers to be powerful Reasons Why. Knowing that, you can stress your own related Reasons Why in your resume and during interviews.

Your Job-Seeker Personal Brand Positioning Statement

Let's check in with our colleagues to see how they have applied their Reasons Why in their Job-Seeker Personal Brand Positioning Statements.

Jamie's Job-Seeker
Personal Brand Positioning Statement

Reasons Why

My Existing Reasons Why (why my Audience should believe I can deliver my Unique Strengths) are:

- *Experience:* Three years of experience working on increasingly complex high-tech DVD design projects at Axion that were strong sellers for Axion's customers and had a 94% success rate for meeting or beating project deadlines.

- *Experience:* At Axion, I on-boarded and trained two new hires.

- *Education:* I have attended a two-day training seminar in 3D DVD design and a week-long training seminar in 3D DVD production.

- *Education:* Bachelors degree in Digital Media, Drexel University.

- *Endorsements:* I have a written reference from my former manager regarding innovative ideas that I suggested and implemented at Axion. This note also talks about my ability to work well with the team, my ability to be self-directed, and my ability to see projects through to completion on schedule.

The Future Reasons Why That I Want to Work on Are:

- *Education:* I will participate in a two-day management seminar in two weeks' time to improve my managerial skills and demonstrate my commitment in this area.

Marcia's Job-Seeker Personal Brand Positioning Statement

Reasons Why

My Existing Reasons Why (why my Audience should believe I can deliver my Unique Strengths) are:

- *Experience:* Ten years total of experience in accounting and seven years as Accounting Manager within a major multinational corporation.

- *Experience:* Examples I can share from my work history with regard to my self-management skills, trustworthiness, ability to make decisions, and superior communication skills.

- *Education:* Certified Public Accountant; Bachelors degree in Accounting from University of Texas-Austin.

The Future Reasons Why That I Want to Work on Are:

- *Endorsements:* Ask current and past colleagues to write references related to my style flexibility, pinpointing my ability to successfully work with a variety of people who have differing backgrounds and ways of behaving.

Do Jamie and Marcia's choices give you some ideas about your own Existing and Future Reasons Why? Take some time to write down your Existing and Future Reasons Why in your Job-Seeker Personal Brand Positioning Statement to prove your Existing and Future Unique Strengths.

YOUR Job-Seeker
Personal Brand Positioning Statement

Reasons Why

My Existing Reasons Why (*why my Audience should believe I can deliver my Unique Strengths*) *are:*

The Future Reasons Why That I Want to Work on Are:

" *Your interviewer has no personal experience of you on the job, so you have to make your Reasons Why both dynamic and believable.* "

"There must be some reason I can never get
an interview here!"

Define it

Inside 6

Character

Step 1

8

Brand Character

Job-Seeker Personal Brand Positioning Element #6

Attitude is a little thing that makes a big difference.
— Winston Churchill, Former British Prime
Minister

T he final positioning element in Step 1 of our system is ... drum roll, please: Brand Character. Why the drum roll? Well, Brand Character may be the last part of your definition, but it definitely isn't the least. Your job-seeker personal Brand Character is incredibly important and can truly differentiate YOU™ from other candidates applying for the job you want. Throughout the whole job search process, Brand Character is something that can and will separate you from other applicants — whether you're just getting your first interview or whether you've been through several rounds and are waiting to be handed the coveted "You're hired!" contract.

But What Exactly Is Brand Character?

When it comes to name brands, you may not have heard of "Brand Character" before. But it definitely exists. And many of the most successful brands out there use Brand Character to differentiate themselves — Pepsi and Coke, for example. Let's be honest: Both Pepsi and Coke are made up of the same basic ingredients — carbonated water, sugar, and flavoring, right? Yet, absolutely everyone seems to have a do-or-die affinity for one over the other. Heck, I've seen people get into big arguments over which cola is "the best!"

With products like Pepsi and Coke that are so similar in ingredients, you can thank their distinctive Brand Characters for the strong brand loyalty people have for them. And the players behind those Brand Characters? The smart Brand Managers who develop and manage those brands. Let's face it: The functional Needs that Pepsi and Coke fill are pretty much the same. They quench your thirst and satisfy your taste buds. But the Brand Character of each of them creates a unique emotional connection that has taken both brands to unbelievable heights in the marketplace. A brand's Character may be less tangible than the Needs it fulfills, but smart Brand Managers take this element of a brand very seriously. It can literally make or break a brand's success.

What are some other brands that are mainly differentiated by Character? Think perfumes, alcohol, and beer just to name a few. Take some time to notice advertising campaigns for these types of brands. For example, what about an ad for Stolichnaya Vodka compared with Cuervo Tequila? The Character of Stoli is older and more traditional, while Cuervo is youthful and focuses on partying with friends. It's actually a lot of fun to discover the Brand Characters that come out in ads and commercials. Keep a watchful eye out for them, and you will clearly see that Brand Character is a critical element that separates one brand from another.

From Pepsi and Vodka to YOU™

So, how does Brand Character apply to you and your personal brand? Your Brand Character is the one element in our six elements that has as much to do with *who* you are as what you do. Think of your personal Brand Character as the "personality" of your brand. While your Unique Strengths are what you offer to your Audience, your personal Brand Character is more about the *way* you offer those Unique Strengths— your attitude and your prevailing temperament.

How do you talk about personal Brand Character? It's most often described with adjectives — the same way you would describe a person. Watch out, though — don't get it confused with a Unique Strength. A Unique Strength is a noun — it's *what* you can offer. To use a brand name example, Duracell battery's Strength might be "longer-lasting," but the Character of the battery brand would be "persistent" or "never gives up."

Are You a Character?

The first task we need to tackle is to figure out your personal Brand Character as it stands right now. In other words, what Brand Character are you currently presenting to others, whether on the job or in your most recent interviews? One of the best ways to determine these Character traits is simply to ask co-workers, friends, and former colleagues what they think your Brand Character is.

You might ask current or past co-workers, as well as people who know you in situations outside of the home, such as your church, community organizations, or places where you volunteer. Their answers will give you a better idea of your personal Brand Character. As always, you want to make sure you ask people you trust. Here are some questions you might ask:

- When you think of me, what are the first descriptive words that come to mind?

- What do you consider to be the most positive aspects of my personality?

- What would you consider to be less positive aspects of my personality?

- If you were trying to sell my Character to someone, what would you tell them?

- If you were writing my obituary, what would you say about me?

Describing Your Character

What adjectives describe your personal Brand Character? Include those you heard from the people you asked, and add in adjectives you think best describe your Brand Character. At first, think about your overall personality rather than just the Character traits you only express at work. The key is to be as specific as possible, and try to think of qualities that aren't the same as everyone else's. Look up words on dictionary.com or thesaurus.com if you need help coming up with more adjectives.

Here are some examples:

Irreverent	Serene	Dedicated
Rascal	Earnest	Even-tempered
Street-wise	Sparkling	Decisive
Authentic	Soulful	Vivacious
Maverick	Eloquent	Generous
Professional	Soft-spoken	Chic
Focused	Gregarious	Spiritual
Gracious	Grounded	Considerate
Altruistic	Industrious	Sociable
Fair-minded	Courageous	Visionary
Colorful	Approachable	Daring
Magnetic	Whimsical	Ethical
Inspirational	Direct	Compassionate
Engaging	Wise	Encouraging
Influential	Persuasive	Passionate

As you think about this list, consider which of these Character traits are most important to you — the most true to the authentic YOU™. How many of your Character traits have you expressed openly and comfortably in your career up to this point? Do you communicate these traits in job interviews?

Another Option: Short Narrative

Besides listing words to describe your personal Brand Character, you can also develop a short narrative that describes your Character. Using a name brand example, the Brand Character of the gargantuan Tide laundry detergent brand could be something like: "The perfectionist who doesn't stop until the job gets done." Switching back to personal branding, YOU™ might be: "The invaluable can-do person you can always count on to take care of what needs to be done." What might be a short narrative descriptor for YOU™?

Let's Get Creative!

You may have hidden some of your personality's strongest characteristics in your work or job interviews, even though these traits could help you get a better job if they were communicated as part of your job-seeker personal brand. Thinking along those lines, let's dig deeper to uncover even more aspects of your Character that can help you in the job search process.

Keep in mind that aspects of your Character can also be developed, but most of the time, your Brand Character is a fundamental part of who you are. For example, Sandra was working as an Administrative Assistant at a medium-sized law firm. She was doing well in her job, but what she really wanted was to be an Administrative Personnel Supervisor in a larger firm with more career advancement opportunities. She learned of a large company that hired fairly regularly for this type of position. But she also learned that the firm looked to their supervisors to continuously develop new ideas for improving office efficiency. Those supervisors were then expected to present those ideas in meetings with managing attorneys. All of this meant Sandra would have to be more assertive on the job than she was used to being. Even though she knew it would be hard for her to assert herself that way, it was something she had always wanted to be able to do. She knew she would have to push herself out of her comfort zone if she wanted to get the job. It wasn't easy, but Sandra was determined.

She decided to work on the Brand Character quality of assertiveness. She became active as a volunteer in her church administration and consciously focused on coming up with ideas that would help the church office run more smoothly. When it came time to share her ideas with others, Sandra had to take a deep breath and muster up the courage, but in the end, several of her ideas were well-received and implemented by the church office with great results. This kind of experience gave Sandra the confidence she needed to try for a job as Administrative Personnel Supervisor at the law firm where she wanted to work. It also gave her several great stories she could tell in interviews about improving the church's office efficiency, even though her stories weren't necessarily related to "work." This edge was enough … and she got the job. "Assertive idea generator and implementer" has simply become a part of Sandra's Character, and it's a valued part of the personal brand that she brings to her new employer.

Creative Comparisons

Sometimes, thinking about the attributes of others will give you ideas of some qualities you might want to focus on or develop in yourself. Here are three ways to open your imagination to other possible descriptive words that you can use for your personal Brand Character.

1. **Compare yourself to a celebrity.** For example:

    Madonna is ... *daring and original* ... and so am I.

    Tiger Woods is ... *focused and dedicated* ... and so am I.

    Oprah Winfrey is ... *charitable and influential* ... and so am I.

    Who could you compare yourself to? Try to think of more than one:

    _____ is _____ and so am I.

2. **Compare yourself to a popular name brand.** For example:

    The clothing brand I am most like is The Gap because ... *I'm trendy and future-thinking.*

    The car brand I am most like is Lamborghini because ... *I'm cutting-edge and state-of-the-art.*

    The bookseller brand I am most like is Amazon.com because ... *I'm fast and have everything at my fingertips.*

    What name brands are you most like?

    The _____ brand I am most like is _____ because I'm _____.

3. **Compare yourself to a role model.** Think of someone you admire from within your local community, such as your Scout leader when you were a child, a favorite teacher, a college advisor, or the mayor of your city.

    *   How would you describe this person? As a leader? As an honorable person?
    *   What characteristics of this individual do you want to develop in yourself?
    *   Is there another role model in your community that you admire? If so, ask yourself the same questions about that person.

Narrowing It Down

As you work on finalizing the personal Brand Character traits you want to develop in yourself, go back and take a look at the Audience you defined in your Job-Seeker Personal Brand Positioning Statement. Does your current personal Brand Character seem to "fit" with the wants, needs, and attitudes of the employers you're targeting? Will it connect with them? If not, which of your other Character traits can you emphasize in future job interviews that will appeal even more to your Audience?

Note that I used the word "appeal." Remember: Personal Brand Character is about the personality, attitude, and prevailing temperament that your Character communicates to others. Will your Audience be *attracted* to your personal Brand Character? This is key when it comes to building a connection with a potential employer and finally finding yourself in that job you've been wanting. If your Brand Character doesn't match what your target companies are looking for, you need to either choose different potential employers or think about adding additional Brand Character traits that are more desirable. Remember, though: YOU™ must be true to who you are. Don't try to turn yourself into someone you're not.

Corporate Brand/Personal Brand— Make the Connection

Sam was an Operations Manager in Great Britain. He loved the meticulous nature of his job—the flow charts and the fishbone diagrams. He prided himself on sticking to strict process guidelines, and that was exactly the type of characteristic that was valued by Sam's company. His superiors knew they could count on Sam for accuracy and that he wouldn't veer off in some direction of his own that could upset the apple cart.

Unfortunately, very suddenly, Sam found himself out of a job when his company filed for bankruptcy and had to drastically reduce its labor force. Even so, since he had many years of experience, Sam felt pretty confident about his job search.

So, it really took him by surprise when his first job interview was a complete disaster! From the very start, Sam could sense the company was just "different" from what he was accustomed to. First of all, the way everyone was dressed was a big clue. They all wore jeans and polo shirts, which immediately made Sam feel uncomfortable and out of place in his finely tailored and pressed suit and tie. He realized he hadn't done the right amount of research to get a better understanding of how this new company operated.

It didn't take him long in the interview to realize that this firm was much more relaxed and "loose" than what he was used to. They obviously wanted employees who were trail-blazers — the types who would do exactly what his former company hated: veer off into new directions. Given Sam's more "stick to the book" approach, this company didn't find Sam's Brand Character in the least bit appealing. The interview turned out to be a discouraging experience for him.

Fortunately for Sam, though, he had a second interview set up a week later with a different company which had a culture that was similar to where he'd been working. They wanted someone like Sam who was meticulous and followed procedures to the letter. Sam immediately resonated with this company's culture (where everyone also wore suits and ties!), and they offered him the job that same afternoon.

What should you take away from Sam's story? Corporations also have a Brand Character all their own. Remember how we've talked about a company's "culture?" If you have worked in more than one place, you know very well that there are definite cultural differences between companies, just as there are cultural differences between countries. If Sam had done some research, he would have found out beforehand that the first firm simply wasn't going to be a good fit for his personal Brand Character. Even if they would have hired him, Sam would have found working there

similar to trying to fit a square peg into a round hole. He could — and should — have avoided wasting time interviewing with that company from the start.

So, take a lesson from Sam, and find out ahead of time if you're spinning your wheels by interviewing with a particular company based on a wrong Brand Character "fit." It will free up that space for an interview with a company that actually suits your Character better.

Reality Check

So, you've done the research on your target companies, and you've evaluated the corporate culture of each. Sit down and look at your list of Brand Character traits, and see which ones are a good fit for your target companies. What have you discovered about each company's Character in your research? Are they a good match with your own personal Brand Character? This is the last piece that can help you decide which of these companies would be a good fit for you.

What happens if you discover that there's a disconnect between your own Brand Character and the Character of a company you've targeted for a job? Well, just like Sam, you may need to sit back and think about whether a real connection with this potential employer (your Audience) is ever truly going to happen. If you would describe your fundamental personal Brand Character as "outgoing, entrepreneurial, innovative, and energetic," for example, but your Audience is looking for someone who is "stable, sticks to status quo, and follows established processes," what would you have to do to make an emotional connection with this Audience? And do you really want to make those changes in your personal Brand Character in order to create that connection, or would it be better for you to spend your energies looking for a job in a company where you know you'd feel more comfortable?

If that's the case, you may have some soul searching to do in terms of how you've been thinking about your job search. You may want to rethink your target companies and look for others that offer more of a "cultural connection" with your Brand Character.

Sometimes, no matter how great a company looks from the outside, your Brand Character may just not be right for it — or the company's Brand Character may just not be right for YOU™!

Bigger Isn't Always Better

In my career coaching work, I've noticed one prevalent trend: Clients often say they want to work for big firms. You know what I mean — the companies with the big names, the big budgets, and the big prestige. But the truth is that many of those companies' Characters don't fit at all with the people who say they want to work for them. I see this over and over again.

The truth is: Well over 90% of all companies in the world are small or medium-sized. That means that the majority of people employed in the world are working for firms that have a smaller number of people working there. So, even though it may seem like it, there are actually not that many truly large companies out there. The bulk of jobs available are within smaller firms. And that means the bulk of the biggest *opportunities* are with smaller firms, too.

Nonetheless, I meet people all the time who tell me they think they should "tough it out" and do the "big company thing" for a while as a resume builder. One of the recruiters I interviewed had the following to say about that: "Most of these people would be happier and do better in their careers if they just found the 'right' company for them instead of worrying about size or name." You can spend a lot of unhappy time trying to prepare for happiness in the future. As Warren Buffet, the "Oracle of Omaha" and Chairman of Berkshire Hathaway, put it, "I always worry about people who say, 'I'm going to do this for ten years [but] I really don't like it very well. And then I'll do this…' That's a little like saving up sex for your old age."

So, remember: Great jobs often come in small packages! Don't overlook smaller companies as excellent places to build your career.

Your Job-Seeker Personal Brand Positioning Statement

As you get ready to fill in the personal Brand Character section of your Job-Seeker Personal Brand Positioning Statement, our fellow job seekers — Jamie and Marcia — have completed theirs as well. Read their personal Brand Character sections, and then choose five to six of the most important qualities (attitudes, character descriptors) you have uncovered to describe YOU™, and add them to your Positioning Statement. These should be the qualities you consider to be your best, as well as the ones you want to develop and grow in order to leapfrog you to "You're hired!"

Jamie's Job-Seeker Personal Brand Positioning Statement

Brand Character

My Personal Brand Character (how I want my Personal Brand Character to be perceived, including my overriding attitude, temperament, and personality) **is:**

A **"Finish Line Champion"** who can supervise, train, and motivate his team through a creative collaborative process to meet or beat customer deadlines.

Marcia's Job-Seeker
Personal Brand Positioning Statement

Brand Character

My Personal Brand Character (how I want my Personal Brand Character to be perceived, including my overriding attitude, temperament, and personality) is:

- Trustworthy and dependable
- Decisive yet involving
- Flexible when it comes to style

What Character do you want to bring to your personal brand? Fill it in to complete the last element of your Job-Seeker Personal Brand Positioning Statement.

YOUR Job-Seeker
Personal Brand Positioning Statement

Brand Character

My Personal Brand Character (how I want my Personal Brand Character to be perceived, including my overriding attitude, temperament, and personality) is:

So, now you've completed Step 1 and defined all six elements of your personal brand. It's time to pull all of the elements together and create a big-picture portrait of your Job-Seeker Personal Brand Positioning Statement.

Step 1

Define it

Outside

1 ▶ Audience

2 ▶ Need

3 ▶ Comparison

▼

Strengths ◀ 4

Why ◀ 5

Character ◀ 6

Inside

9

Pulling It All Together

Your Complete Job-Seeker
Personal Brand Positioning Statement

Details create the big picture.

— Sanford I. Weill, Banker, financier
and philanthropist

W ell done! You've defined all six elements of your personal brand and filled in all of the boxes in your Job-Seeker Personal Brand Positioning Statement. Now, it's time to pull it all together into a clear and consistent "big picture."

Before we do, though, let's take a look at the completed Job-Seeker Personal Brand Positioning Statements of Jamie and Marcia. I encourage you to read them this time with an overall sense of each of their job-seeker personal brands.

Jamie's Job-Seeker
Personal Brand Positioning Statement

Audience

My Audience is: PreLife, a multimedia firm that is expanding into 3D DVD design.

Company Facts: PreLife is a company with about 150 employees located a 25-minute drive from where I live. The company was founded in 1999 and has grown fairly rapidly. The DVD department is one of the fastest growing areas of the company, and the focus on 3D design is just now starting.

Company Culture: PreLife is all about innovation and creativity. They have a track record of hiring younger employees because the company finds fresh new ideas just as important as experience. The company has no problem hiring a manager in his or her 20's as long as the person in question demonstrates management potential.

Department Culture: The DVD department is interested in managers who can take the reins of projects and run with them, making sure no existing clients are lost during the new staff's learning curve. The culture is also very much a team atmosphere, where everyone's input is valued. PreLife makes it a point to hire people who are creative, so everyone has the potential to contribute. But the company has grown so fast that a lot of new employees need to be trained; for example, they're behind in getting everyone up to speed on the new 3D DVD design process and how the new area of focus will run effectively.

Interviewer: I will be interviewing with Tom Brunnell, the 30-year old manager of the new 3D DVD department. He has been with the company for four years. From Tom's LinkedIn.com profile, I can see he is very well liked because there are recommendations from some of the employees he manages. Tom calls himself a "computer geek" in his profile and says that he just can't get enough of technical knowledge. This is something I have in common with him. He graduated from Georgia Institute of Technology and spent four years working for a small (now defunct) digital media company, first as a team member, then as an Assistant Manager.

Needs

Functional: An independent-thinking 3D DVD development team leader who can stimulate his team to deliver innovative ideas that satisfy the customer's desired specifications while meeting or beating project deadlines.

Someone experienced enough in 3D DVD design to train staff members who are relatively new to this type of design.

Emotional: Someone Tom can count on to successfully implement new design ideas without a lot of hand-holding or supervision.

Comparison

Job Title: Assistant Manager - 3D DVD Department

Desired Identity: I *want* to be the brand of **"Finish Line Champion"** — A reliable Assistant Manager who takes the reins at the starting line and motivates the team through the race, getting the project to the finish line in record time.

Unique Strengths

My Existing Unique Strengths are:

- Provider of truly new and innovative ideas in multimedia design that satisfy customers' needs and meet or beat project deadlines.
- Demonstrated ability to train others in DVD design.
- Strong history of self-management.

The Future Unique Strengths That I Want to Work on Are:

- Team leadership and management skills — ability to take a small group of people forward and make creative decisions, especially when there is little time for on-the-spot direction.

Reasons Why

My Existing Reasons Why are:

- *Experience:* Three years experience working on increasingly complex high-tech DVD design projects at Axion that were strong sellers for Axion's customers and had a 94% success rate for meeting or beating project deadlines.

- *Experience:* At Axion, I on-boarded and trained two new hires.

- *Education:* I have attended a two-day training seminar in 3D DVD design and a week-long training seminar in 3D DVD production.

- *Education:* Bachelors degree in Digital Media, Drexel University.

- *Endorsements:* I have a written reference from my former manager regarding innovative ideas that I suggested and implemented at Axion. This note also talks about my ability to work well with the team, my ability to be self-directed, and my ability to see projects through to completion on schedule.

The Future Reasons Why That I Want to Work on Are:

- *Education:* I will participate in a two-day management seminar in two weeks' time to improve my managerial skills and demonstrate my commitment in this area.

Brand Character

My Personal Brand Character is:

A **"Finish Line Champion"** who can supervise, train, and motivate his team through a creative collaborative process to meet or beat customer deadlines.

"Pay attention! You're my target Audience!"

Marcia's Job-Seeker Personal Brand Positioning Statement

Audience

My Audience is: Samson Foods International

Company Facts: Currently, this company has almost 17,000 employees across multiple offices in North America, Europe, and Asia. The company has dozens of well-known brands and is growing. In fact, to accommodate this growth, the company recently expanded its offices to an additional floor in its headquarters here and is opening two new offices overseas right now as well. The Snacks Division is among the fastest growing divisions of the company, and that's where the company is looking to add talent.

Company Culture: I was told in my first interview that the corporation values loyalty and looks for people who want to commit long term. They believe in offering their employees the same kind of loyalty, which includes a fair number of incentives and assistance, such as training opportunities, chances for advancement, an onsite cafeteria at discounted prices, annual bonuses, and two holiday parties — one for the adults and one for children of employees. It's a buttoned-down atmosphere, with everyone dressed very professionally and sticking to fairly strict but unwritten "look" guidelines.

Interviewer: Bina Tilak was promoted to Vice President of Finance about one year ago after five years of holding the position I'm applying for. In the press release about Bina's promotion, I read into it that Bina is a no-nonsense go-getter who expects a lot of her staff because she expects a lot of herself. From my first interview with the company, I found out that Bina is a bit of a perfectionist, and I get a sense she has a tendency to micro-manage her direct reports. From what the HR rep told me, I think Bina may have some "trust" issues since it appears that the former Accounting Director made some poor decisions without consulting Bina that negatively impacted the division.

Needs

Functional: A self-directed Accounting Director with the experience to delve right into the job with minimal training in the corporation's procedures.

A great communicator who will keep the VP of Finance up-to-date at all times as to what's going on.

Emotional: Reliability — Someone Bina can finally rely upon to take charge of the job quickly and seamlessly so that she can truly attend to her position as Vice President.

Trust — Someone Tilak can be assured has good judgment and will know when to involve Bina when big decisions need to be made.

Comparison

Job Title: Accounting Director – Snacks Division

Desired Identity: I *want* to be the brand of **"Experienced, Trusted Communicator"** who uses good judgment to make sure work is done efficiently and accurately and who always communicates fully with the VP of Finance.

Unique Strengths

My Existing Unique Strengths are:

- Outstanding accounting experience and credentials.
- Strong self-management skills.
- Clear and regular communicator.
- Reliable and trusted decision-maker.

The Future Unique Strengths That I Want to Work on Are:

- Adjusting style to work well with a boss who is more of a micro-manager.

Reasons Why

My Existing Reasons Why are:

- *Experience:* Ten years total of experience in accounting and seven years as Accounting Manager within a major multinational corporation.

- *Experience:* Examples I can share from my work history with regard to my self-management skills, trustworthiness, ability to make decisions, and superior communication skills.

- *Education:* Certified Public Accountant; Bachelors degree in Accounting from University of Texas-Austin.

The Future Reasons Why That I Want to Work on Are:

- *Endorsements:* Ask current and past colleagues to write references related to my style flexibility, pinpointing my ability to successfully work with a variety of people with differing backgrounds and ways of behaving.

Brand Character

My Personal Brand Character is:

- Trustworthy and dependable
- Decisive yet involving
- Flexible when it comes to style

Reading through their examples, do you see how the elements of Jamie and Marcia's statements all fit together? Do you think their statements could be improved? If you were sitting at a coffee shop with either of our job seekers, and they asked you for feedback, what input would you give them?

Now, one more time, read through your own completed Job-Seeker Personal Brand Positioning Statement. As you review it, try to look at it objectively. If you were an outsider reading through it, what advice or recommendations would you give to YOU™?

YOUR Job-Seeker
Personal Brand Positioning Statement

Audience

My Audience is:

Company Facts:

Company Culture:

Division/Department Culture:

Interviewer:

Potential Boss/Supervisor:

Needs

Functional:

Emotional:

Comparison

Job Title:

Desired Identity: I *want* to be the brand of:

Unique Strengths

My Existing Unique Strengths are:

The Future Unique Strengths That I Want to Work on Are:

Reasons Why

My Existing Reasons Why are:

The Future Reasons Why That I Want to Work on Are:

Brand Character

My Personal Brand Character is:

Is Your Statement Complete?

As you sit back and look at the work you've done, be sure to double-check that your Positioning Statement has all of the information it needs:

1. **Audience**
   - Does your statement have all of the elements of a well-defined Audience? When you read it, do you really feel you "know" what your target companies are all about?

2. **Needs**
   - Are the Needs listed the ones you honestly believe to be the most important ones for this prospective employer?
   - Did you list both functional and emotional Needs of your Audience?

3. **Comparison**
   - Is your Desired Identity clearly defined and unique?
   - Is it unique and different enough that it can help you stand out from other job applicants?

4. **Unique Strengths**
   - Do you have 1-4 clear Unique Strengths that you know you want to — and can — own? If you have more than four, are they truly the most important Strengths for YOU™?
   - Do your Unique Strengths respond to both the functional and emotional Needs of your Audience?

5. **Reasons Why**
   - Are your Reasons Why strong enough to be convincing to your Audience? Will they really help to prove you can deliver the Unique Strengths you've outlined for yourself?
   - Do you need some Future Reasons Why to better support the Future Unique Strengths you want to develop in yourself?

6. **Personal Brand Character**

- Is your personal Brand Character in sync with what you've found out about the culture and the values of the companies you're targeting?
- Based on what you know about your target companies, is your stated Brand Character going to appeal to that Audience?

How Does It Look?

So, all in all, how do you feel about your job-seeker personal brand now that you can sit back and see the big picture? Does it feel "right" to you? Is your statement on target, and does it accurately tell your story? On a scale from 1 to 10, how well does your statement really communicate who YOU™ are and who YOU™ want to be? If you don't think you can score your statement at around at least an 8 or 9, take some more time to think about the various elements to see how you might improve your personal brand definition. It's fundamental to get this part right, so be sure to devote the time you need to feel as good about your job-seeker personal brand as possible.

It could be that you can't score your statement as high as you'd like because you have some work to do yet on your job-seeker personal brand. Did you find some gaps between your Existing Unique Strengths, Reasons Why, and Brand Character traits and the ones you truly need in order to get your ultimate job? Maybe you realize that the Future Reasons Why or personal Brand Character traits that you want to work on will take you a fair amount of time.

If this is the case, don't get discouraged! Even if the job you really want seems to be far off in the future, focus on getting an important interim job to help you get there. In fact, find out if the companies you are targeting have a dream position that you can work toward. If there's room for advancement there, you can aim for a lower-level position and develop your personal brand from within the company. That will help you move through the ranks as you add to your Unique Strengths, Reasons Why, and Brand Character traits. In the meantime, get a better start at your new company by kicking it off with a powerhouse personal brand that is as close as possible to your desired, longer-term personal brand.

Get Feedback

Before you sign off on your Positioning Statement, get some objective opinions.

- Show your Job-Seeker Personal Brand Positioning Statement to others you trust, and ask for their feedback. If you know any recruiters or HR professionals (whether or not they work in your field), they can help by commenting on your statement. Do they agree it presents a great personal brand for you, knowing what they know about you? Do they think the vision for your brand is strong enough to help you get the type of job, salary, and recognition you're looking for?

- Feeling a bit daring? If so, you could even e-mail or call a person who interviewed you in the past but didn't offer you a job, and ask that person for a few minutes of friendly feedback. You could tell that person how you had hoped to come across in your interviews as hardworking, loyal, and good-natured (or whatever brand characteristics are appropriate to YOU™) and ask how well you succeeded at that. By the way, I don't recommend you share your entire Positioning Statement with this person, but just mention how you had hoped to come across in the interview. This will help you do better the next time.

- Visit www.HowYOUAreLikeShampoo.com and, for a small fee, you can download a helpful "e-audit" form that will walk you through a number of additional questions to think about as you finalize and review your Job-Seeker Personal Brand Positioning Statement. We also offer one-on-one professional coaching sessions by phone to discuss your Personal Brand Positioning Statement. Visit www.HowYOUAreLikeShampoo.com for more information.

Now, it's time to move on to Step 2 of our system where you'll discover what you need to do to best communicate your job-seeker personal brand before, during, and after job interviews.

" *So, all in all, how do you feel about your job-seeker personal brand now that you can sit back and see the big picture? Does it feel 'right' to you?* "

"Hire the woman in there selling maps!"

10

Taking YOU™ On Interviews

We would rather be in the company of somebody we like than in the company of the most superior being of our acquaintance.

— Frank Swinnerton, English critic and novelist

Here's a startling truth about interviews:

The best, most qualified candidate doesn't always get the job. It's the best *interviewee* who almost always gets the job.

No matter how great your resume, if you don't communicate your personal brand effectively in the job interview, there's a good chance you'll be out of luck — and, unfortunately, out of a job.

This happens time and again. A great candidate on paper may have trouble getting a job because he or she just isn't all that good at interviewing. It can be incredibly frustrating to candidates who aren't chosen when they know their qualifications are perfect for the job. But if they've spent more time perfecting their resume than focusing on how to define and communicate the great job-seeker personal brand they want to communicate in their interviews, their qualifications may simply not be enough.

The Likeability Factor

Here's another stark reality: Interviewers hire people they like. In fact, some recruiters estimate that as much as 40% of the hiring decision is based on whether or not you were liked in your interview.

If you think about it, this is also the case with name brands. After all, you buy name brands you like, right? The same holds true on the job. Don't you prefer to work with people you like?

It's no different with employers. They hire people they believe they will like working with, and YOU™ are no exception. The truth is: Interviewers will hire you because they like you and because you've made a connection with them.

This is where Step 2 of our job-seeker personal branding system comes in. It will show you how to intelligently and effectively communicate your personal brand in interviews. It will teach you how to be a great interviewee and to really connect with your interviewers. That's what personal branding is all about — communicating who YOU™ really are.

Bring On the Heavy Interview Artillery

Yes, I know that interviews are stressful, but there is an entire arsenal of things you can do to feel more confident and master the interview process. The upcoming chapters will outline the five core activities that are designed to help you have non-stop successful interview experiences and — yes — walk away from interviewers knowing that you were "liked." This is how to make sure the best parts of YOU™ are communicated in the strongest way possible to potential employers. And that, of course, leads to your ultimate objective: an inspiring, exciting new job.

That's what personal branding is all about — communicating who YOU™ really are.

Communicate it

Actions

11

Launching Your Job-Seeker Personal Brand

All paths lead to the same goal: to convey to others what we are.
— Pablo Neruda, Chilean poet

P ablo Neruda's above quote is certainly true, especially when it comes to personal brands. Of course, in our case, it's about how you want to be viewed by potential employers. But no matter how brilliant the job-seeker personal brand you have defined, it will remain useless unless you communicate it to the people who are making the hiring decisions — and that means from the moment your resume crosses their desk to your first interview to your follow-up communications.

It's incredibly important to communicate your job-seeker personal brand *consistently* throughout the entire job search process. Only then will YOU™ make the leap from a concept in your mind to a perception in the mind of your Audience that is exactly what you want it to be. Then, you and YOU™ will be interchangeable before, during, and after your job interviews. This is what will help you take control of your career, land the great job you're after, achieve the recognition you desire and deserve, and increase the balance in your bank account.

Your Personal Brand's Coming-Out Party

Your personal brand should come out into the open so that it can do what you want it to do — get you the job you want. So, the question is: How do you communicate the job-seeker personal brand you've worked so hard to define?

Let's take a look at how successful name brands communicate their brands to their Target Market. Sit back for a moment, and think of one brand in particular that you feel strongly about — a brand that you use regularly and that you have a powerful connection with. How has this particular brand communicated to you what it stands for? How has it made clear to you the elements of its Positioning Statement? How has this brand found its way through your pocketbook and into your heart?

Perhaps you're loyal to Colgate toothpaste. Maybe you like the taste, and with regular use, you haven't had a cavity in five years. Did your brother-in-law come out of a rollover accident without a bruise while driving a Volvo? Do you take your kids to McDonald's because of the Happy Meals and the playgrounds?

What these examples show is that a big name brand communicates its positioning to you via what it *does*, not by what it says it is. Think about it: You've never seen McDonald's Brand Positioning Statement, right? And the brand manager at Toyota isn't likely to invite you to dinner in order to show you the definition of Toyota's Brand Character. That would be absurd! No, the *experience* you have with a specific brand is what most communicates its positioning statement.

As we mentioned before, the true key to success of any brand is how consistently it communicates what it does. For example, Volvo wouldn't sponsor a demolition derby, but it would sponsor a family safety day. Nike wouldn't support an online computer game contest targeted at teens, but it would support a charity marathon. To be consistent in their communications, Volvo will continue to focus on safety in everything it presents to the public, and Nike will regularly communicate its "Just Do It" attitude to its sports-loving audience. This kind of consistency is the Holy Grail when it comes to positioning a brand in the marketplace.

It's the same with personal brands. I can show you my Personal Brand Positioning Statement, and I can tell you that's what I stand for, but you will make decisions on my personal brand based on what I do, not based on what I say.

The Five Activities That Communicate Your Job-Seeker Personal Brand

Now you know that your personal brand is communicated by what you do. But "what you do" is a pretty big category. I have interviewed hundreds of folks in corporations throughout the world, and I have spoken with dozens of recruiters and human resources professionals, asking them how applicants can best communicate their personal brands. As a result, I firmly believe there are five core activities you do before, during, and after every job interview that most communicate your job-seeker personal brand:

> Your ... **Actions**
>
> Your ... **Reactions**
>
> Your ... **Look**
>
> Your ... **Sound**
>
> Your ... **Thoughts**

I really believe these five activities are responsible for 99% of how a potential employer perceives, thinks, and feels about YOU™. These five activities are critical to success in the interviewing process. They are how you will showcase your job-seeker personal brand to a company where you want to work.

All That—In the Short Span of an Interview?

Now, you may be thinking, "But, Brenda, I'm only in a job interview for a short time. How much can I actually do to communicate my personal brand in less than a half hour?" No matter how much time you have with the interviewer, I will show you how you can use all five of these activities to best communicate your job-seeker personal brand. You can absolutely communicate your personal brand in the span of a few minutes. In fact, you'll see that you begin communicating your brand as soon as your resume and cover letter leave your e-mail outbox or as soon as they arrive in the company's mail!

But let's not get ahead of ourselves. We're going to devote the next five chapters to each of these five activities, so you'll have plenty of time to learn how to master each one. No marketing plan would be complete, though, without a clear positioning summary to start us off.

Your Job-Seeker Personal Brand Marketing Plan

Remember the Job-Seeker Personal Brand Marketing Plan I mentioned at the beginning of the book? Just like successful name brands have full-blown marketing plans to make sure they communicate their messages consistently via TV commercials, magazine ads, sponsored events, their website, the brand's packaging, public relations efforts, etc., so the five activities we're going to talk about are your own "media" of sorts when it comes to your own Job-Seeker Personal Brand Marketing Plan. These five activities are how you communicate to a potential employer who YOU™ really are — whether it's during a phone conversation to set up an interview or in a face-to-face meeting.

If you're serious about how you want a potential company to perceive, think, and feel about you, keep these five activities top of mind every single day throughout your job search to make sure you are absolutely consistent in conveying your job-seeker personal brand. And whether you're currently employed or not, you never know when you might meet someone who could help you get your next great job. So, it's important to be consistent all the time — not just during your interviews. Keep the five activities in mind in every situation.

The Job-Seeker Personal Brand Marketing Plan Format

Let's look at the Job-Seeker Personal Brand Marketing Plan format. On the left side, you will put a brief summary of your Job-Seeker Personal Brand Positioning Statement. On the right, you will decide which elements of the five activities you need to work on in order to better communicate your job-seeker personal brand throughout the job search process.

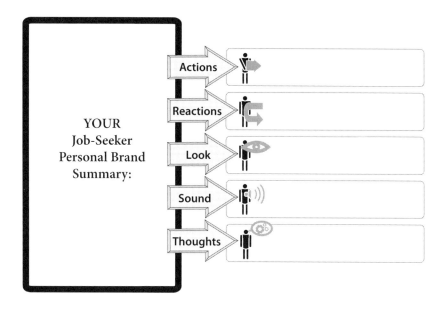

First, you'll want to develop an overall positioning summary of your personal brand. What is that? Well, think of your personal brand positioning summary as the brief "bottom line" — a short statement that pulls together the core of what YOU™ want to stand for.

How do you write this? Look again at the different parts of your Job-Seeker Personal Brand Positioning Statement, and come up with what you think is the heart of the personal brand you want to communicate. Your summary statement might come from your Brand Character, your Unique Strengths, your Desired Label, your Reasons Why — or maybe a combination of one or more of these.

Let's take a look at what job seekers Jamie and Marcia have chosen for their job-seeker personal brand positioning summaries. This can help you get a sense of how the summary looks and sounds.

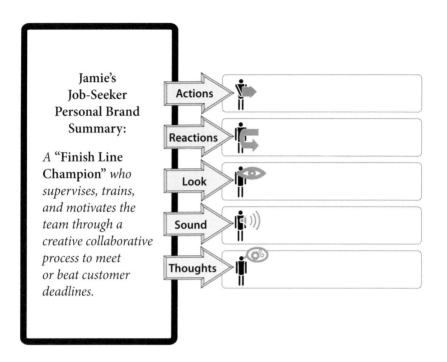

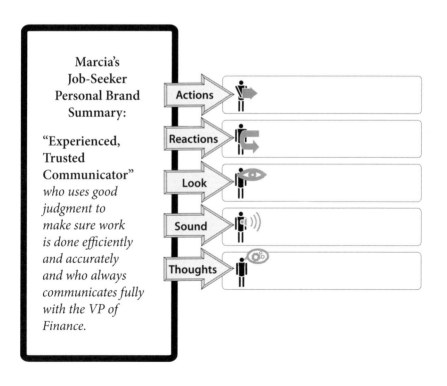

Hopefully, you can see how the summaries of Jamie and Marcia briefly and simply encapsulate what they want their job-seeker personal brands to stand for. Now, go ahead and add your own personal brand summary to the left of your Job-Seeker Personal Brand Marketing Plan. At the end of each of the next five chapters, you'll be able to add your own ideas about how you plan to leverage the five Marketing Plan activities.

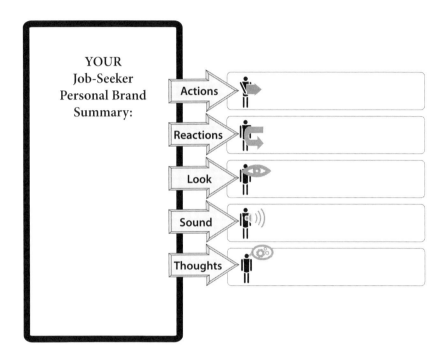

Step 2
Communicate it

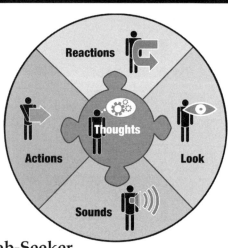

Job-Seeker
Personal Brand Marketing Plan

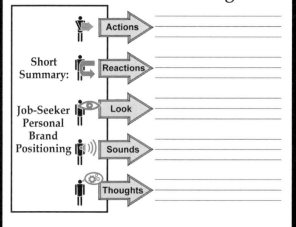

12

Actions

Job-Seeker Personal Brand Marketing Plan Activity #1

As I grow older, I pay less attention to what men say. I just watch what they do.

— Andrew Carnegie, Founder of the U.S. steel industry

The first activity in your Job-Seeker Personal Brand Marketing Plan is your Actions. You may think that all five of the activities that make up your Personal Brand Marketing Plan are "actions," but in this case, what I mean by Actions are behaviors others can see that can influence the way your personal brand is communicated. Think of it as how you conduct yourself — your overall manner. This includes how you handle yourself on the phone, via e-mails or letters, during an interview, etc.

You may not even be aware of some of your Actions, but they can have a huge impact on the way a potential employer perceives, thinks, and feels about you.

No matter how great your background, your personal brand will take a hit if your Actions put off an interviewer. Think for a second about people you've met. Have you ever spoken to someone on the phone who hung up without saying goodbye? What was your impression of that person? Maybe you know someone who is very smart and capable but never looks you in the eye. It can come across as a lack of interest or lack of confidence. These kinds of Actions influence the way your job-seeker personal brand is perceived by that key person or group of people who are considering you for a job.

The Actions we're talking about can be either social or directly related to the job. When you think about it, interviewing for a job is kind of a combination of the two, isn't it? It's definitely a work-related meeting, but it's also somewhat of a "social" meeting, too, where you and the interviewer get to know each other as people. That's why your Actions are judged in an interview both in terms of your experience and suitability for the job, as well as how much the interviewer likes you and gets along with you.

So, we know Actions are an important part of a successful job search and critical to communicating your job-seeker personal brand in an interview, but how can you take control of your Actions — especially if you're not even conscious of them?

Seeing Yourself Through the Eyes of an Employer

It's important to try to see yourself the way a potential employer sees you, but that isn't always easy. You're inside yourself, so it's hard to know how your Actions "read" to others on the outside. But figuring out which of your Actions might be helping your personal brand — and which ones might be hurting it — is an important key to the success of your job search.

The first step to seeing yourself through the eyes of someone who might hire you is to really know your Audience. The work you've already done to understand your Audience and what they need will be incredibly helpful at this stage. After completing the Audience portion of your Job-Seeker Personal Brand Positioning Statement, you should have a pretty good sense of the Actions your target companies would look for in a candidate.

In fact, take time now to go back and review the Audience section of your Positioning Statement. Think about what Actions your target companies would value most. Include both work behaviors and social behaviors. For example, if you know a company values reliability, what Actions will you focus on demonstrating in your interview? You will want to always show up on time, call back exactly at the time you've been asked to call, follow up with the interviewer with regard to any unanswered questions from the interview, etc.

But your Actions don't just affect how your job-seeker personal brand is perceived while you're sitting across from the interviewer.

There are Actions you can take before and after your interview as well that will have an impact on your job search.

Your Actions *Before* the Interview

The Actions you need to think about before an interview are usually related to the following: (1) communicating with a target company prior to the interview via phone calls, e-mails, your cover letter, and your resume, and (2) preparation for the moment you step into the company's offices. You'll want to take each of these into account before every one of your interviews.

Network, Network, Network. How many times have you heard about the importance of networking when it comes to looking for a job ... dozens? hundreds? Well, there's a reason. Hiring experts estimate that as many as 60% to 75% of all jobs are found through networking as opposed to job postings. Without a doubt, it's one of the most effective ways to find a job.

What does this mean for YOU™? Pick up the phone, make connections with anyone and everyone you can, and let them know you're interested in a new job. E-mail family, e-mail friends, and e-mail friends of friends (where appropriate). This can be a bit of a challenge if you tend to be on the shy side, but it's important to take a deep breath, swallow your fears, and get the word out.

Throw the net wide. Think of all of the people you could contact from former co-workers, former bosses, subordinates, classmates, and vendors to friends, family, acquaintances, past clients, and people you know through associations and your community. Brainstorm as many contacts as you can. Make connections through Facebook.com, LinkedIn.com, and other online networks as well.

Send Resumes to Your Favorite Companies. Apply directly to the target employers you identify through your sleuthing and networking. Yes, networking is a great way to find a job, but the United States Census Bureau found that, at least in the U.S., applying directly to employers can be one of the most effective ways people find a new job. It doesn't matter if the company hasn't placed a want ad. Considering this data, if you only have a limited time for your job search, it probably makes the most sense to spend the majority of your time networking and sending resumes to the companies you'd most like to work with — whether or not you know if they have any openings. If you do so, the statistics of finding a job via those two means is in your favor.

Don't Stop There. Of course, even though networking and applying directly to employers are the most successful means of getting hired, they're not the only way to land the job you want. While you may focus the majority of your energy on these methods, don't forget that you're on a job-seeking personal brand mission! That means you will want to use every way possible to get the job that is just right for YOU™. So, check online job summaries, read the want ads in the newspaper, check with employment agencies and headhunters (including private and government-run agencies), and check with college placement offices. Don't leave any stone unturned when it comes to your job search!

Stay Organized. As Nora Bammann, Assistant Human Resources Manager of The Kroger Company, says: "One of the most important parts of any job search is to adopt an organized approach. I will only provide names of networking contacts to job seekers who seem to have a good grasp on how to present themselves professionally and who can explain to me clearly what they've already done to try and get good results in their job search. All of us are extremely busy, and I don't want to recommend someone to my colleagues or contacts if it's just going to be a waste of their time."

Want to get more organized while searching for a job? Here are some tips you can start using right away to help you stay on top of your job search:

- Create file folders or an online filing system to keep track of all of the Actions you're taking during your job search.

- Keep notes — in a binder or on your computer — about all of the people you meet, each company that you target, each job, and each interview.

- Include the time and date when you spoke with each individual, a brief summary of what was said, and what "next steps" were indicated, if any.

- Keep a list of the proper spelling of names, including the names of receptionists and assistants (so that you can call them by name when you arrive for an interview or if you need to follow up with them). Include job titles on your list, too.

This may seem like a lot of work, but trust me — it works! Take Robin, for example, an advertising agency planner who has been with her current company for two years: "The details I wrote down about my interviews were what eventually helped me to get the job I have now," she says. "You see, my current company took a long time to get back to me after my initial interview with them, and by the time they did, I had been through at least a dozen other interviews with different companies. If I hadn't kept such good notes from that first interview, I wouldn't have been able to remember the discussion I had with the person who interviewed me. As it was, the interviewer was so impressed with my ability to pick up the conversation where we left off that she told me that was one of the key reasons she hired me over the other candidates they were considering."

Your Cover Letter and Resume. If you're like most people, you've probably put in a lot of work perfecting just the right cover letter. And you've dotted every "i" and crossed every "t" of your resume, right? But how do you really know these documents are perfect for YOU™?

Here's a great exercise to help you see how others might view your cover letter or resume: Print out a copy of what you think is your very best cover letter, attach your resume, fold it up, put it in an envelope, and mail it to yourself. When it arrives in your mailbox a couple of days later, pretend you've never laid eyes on either one of these documents before. Open them up, and look at them objectively. What is your initial impression? Go back to your personal brand summary and remind yourself of how you want a potential employer to perceive, think, and feel about you. Are these documents truly "working" for YOU™?

Put yourself in the shoes of a potential employer. What would you think of someone who sends you an impersonal form cover letter that has obviously been sent to many other companies? Or how about receiving a cryptic resume with little information about the applicant's experience? Wouldn't that be a very different personal brand from someone who provides you with a cover letter that talks about the specific position that person wants and offers knowledgeable details about the target division and company?

What about a resume that speaks specifically about how someone implemented new ideas and projects at their previous company?

In the same vein, how would you feel about someone who presents you with an excessively long and wordy resume, going on and on about how they single-handedly created every project their previous company implemented in the last several years? Which one of these people would you most likely choose to hire? All of them may have the same desired personal brand of "the go-to person for innovative ideas," but the Actions that these individuals take with their cover letters and resumes will have a big impact on how their job-seeker personal brands are communicated.

Apply the 80-for-20 Rule. Maybe you've been procrastinating getting your resume out there because it isn't quite "ready" yet. If that's the case, follow Nike's advice and "just do it." You definitely don't want to have any avoidable mistakes on your resume — like typos, incorrect dates, or misspelled words — but even a less-than-perfect resume is better in the hands of someone who might hire you than it is sitting on your desk waiting until it's "100% ready."

When coaching clients through career changes, I've found that waiting for a resume to be "perfect" is often just a sign of fear raising its ugly head and manipulating you into procrastination. But fear and procrastination won't get you the job you want. So, live by the 80-for-20 rule when it comes to your resume: "If it's 80% done, then it's good enough — consider it done." You can always make slight adjustments as you receive feedback, but the key is to just get your resume out there where it can be working to get you an interview now!

Practice Great E-mail Etiquette. In your job search, it's very important to be conscious of good e-mail etiquette. In these days of phone texting and quick "one-liner" e-mails, it's easy to forget that e-mail is actually a replacement for the old-fashioned letter. If you were sending a letter in an envelope via the post office to a potential employer, how would it look and what would you say? Do your e-mails look the same? For example, try to include the name and title of your interviewer in your e-mails, and make sure you spell the name right. Begin every e-mail just like you would a cover letter with "Dear _____." End each e-mail with "Sincerely" or "Best regards." Remember: Every piece of communication you have with a potential employer plays a role in how that employer will perceive, think, and feel about your job-seeker personal brand.

Anticipate Questions. Sit down and brainstorm every possible question you think an interviewer might ask you, and prepare your answers. Well thought-out responses will show you've spent time thinking about your accomplishments and strengths — and that builds a strong personal brand image. Even if an interviewer asks a question you didn't think of beforehand, you will feel more confident if you're ready with answers to most every question you've brainstormed.

You will also want to check out Appendix A at the end of this book for a list of great questions supplied by Sigmund Ginsburg, Executive Search Consultant from DHR International's New York office. These are terrific questions from a recruiting expert that you should be prepared to answer in any interview.

Make Lists for Each Interview. Prior to each of your interviews, make three separate lists:

1. List the key points you want to get across in the interview about your experience, your education, and how you "fit" with the job you're seeking. You can base this on what you discovered in your investigations about the company's expectations, values, and Needs.

2. Develop a second list that outlines all of the information about the job or the company that you don't currently know. Split this list into two: (a) the information you feel you *need* to know in order to decide if the job is right for you, and (b) the information you feel you would *like* to know but that isn't critical to know.

3. Based on your lists of what you need to know or would like to know, make a final list of the questions you want to ask during your upcoming interview about the job or the company. Here, prioritizing is key because you may only be given enough time to ask one question. With that in mind, if you really do get to ask only one question about the job or the company, what will it be? If you have time to ask just two questions, which two will they be? Again, remember that they may be the only questions you have time to ask in the interview, so make them pertinent.

In Appendix A, Sig Ginsburg doesn't just give you the questions you should be prepared to answer. He also offers you several questions to consider asking the interviewer. While you're putting together your three lists, take a look at Sig's questions to give you some ideas.

Practice, Practice, Practice. Now that you know how you would answer just about every imaginable question, a key to your success is to practice. Enlist a friend's help, and write each question on a piece of paper. If you can find someone who actually conducts interviews regularly, you will receive the best possible feedback. Have your friend ask you each of the questions in rapid-fire succession. Then, ask your friend for honest feedback and insights about how well you answered each question. Did you answer the questions to their satisfaction and in a way that communicated your personal brand well?

Videotape Yourself in a Mock Interview, if Possible. Get another friend to play interviewer, asking you those same questions you think you'll be asked. Then, sit back and watch yourself on tape. This is one of the best ways to learn how you're coming across in a potential interview, and it can be a real eye opener. In all honesty, it may not be something you enjoy (does anybody really like watching themselves on film?), but it will almost certainly show you what you need to work on in order to improve the way you're perceived by an interviewer.

Get Truly Objective Feedback. Once you've videotaped your mock interview, ask someone who doesn't know you very well to watch the tape and give you feedback as to what they perceive, think, and feel about YOU™ based on the video. This is such a good learning experience, and it will be your strongest clue about whether you're communicating your job-seeker personal brand through your Actions or not.

Communicate Your Personal Brand to Everyone. Don't forget: Your personal brand needs to be communicated to everyone you encounter in the interview process from your first phone call or e-mail to the moment you walk in the door of the company to your last phone call or e-mail. This includes any headhunters/employment agents as well. Think about it: These agencies represent you, so if they don't get a clear sense of your brand, how can they help you find the job you want? Recruiters and employment agencies have a reputation to maintain with their client companies, so they won't be enthusiastic to sell you if they don't feel they know YOU™. This means that your Actions must demonstrate to these folks exactly how you will come across in an interview.

What Signals Do You Send? Become as aware as you can of the signals your Actions send. Of course, remember that different people interpret Actions in different ways. For example, let's say that Victoria has talked to a few people who actually know her prospective boss. Through these inside talks, she has found out that one of her potential boss's core Needs is *precision*. For her interview, Victoria has been asked to bring a portfolio showing her work as a civil engineer, complete with her own past case studies.

- If Victoria arrives with her portfolio in an attractive folder with the case studies printed out and well-organized, that's a very different "precise" brand than …

- If Victoria arrives with her case studies in a random pile of papers out of order. She brought the requested materials, and each one of them may actually be very exact on its own, but that's yet a very different "precise" brand than …

- If Victoria shows up with some handwritten notes and no real portfolio … well, that's not really a "precise" brand at all, is it?

Never Forget Your Personal Brand! Right before arriving for the interview, remember who YOU™ are by keeping your personal brand positioning summary top of mind. Go back over your personal brand key attributes and the definitions you've developed in your Job-Seeker Personal Brand Positioning Statement. You might even type up a small reminder and stick it in your pocket so that you can review it immediately before walking into the interviewer's office.

Your Actions *During* the Interview

Your hard work and pre-interview Actions paid off, and you got the call to set up a meeting with the HR Department. Now, it's the day of the interview. You arrive at the company's location, and it's the moment of truth. You're walking into the building where the interview will take place. This particular interview is for the job you really want, so it's critical to make sure your Actions communicate your job-seeker personal brand from the moment you step into the company's offices to the moment you walk away from the building. What will be your first Action? It might be introducing yourself to the security guard or the receptionist. Maybe it will be a handshake with one of these people. Here are some ways that you can make sure YOU™ perform like the strong brand you want.

Always Be Courteous. Let's face it: "Nice" works! Are you pleasant to everyone you speak with from the minute you walk in the door? Don't treat the receptionist or the security guard with impatience on the phone or in person. That kind of Action could very easily get back to your potential employer and spoil your chances of being hired.

If you enter a room with a smile and your hand extended for a warm handshake, it communicates that you're happy to be there. Even if you're nervous, presenting a friendly attitude will very likely reduce your anxiety, especially since others are more likely to respond in kind and help put you at ease.

How's Your Handshake? Don't underestimate the importance of your handshake! In most interview situations, before you even open your mouth or hand out your business card, you're making a first impression with your grip. Trust me: Your interviewer is going to judge your level of confidence based on your handshake. With that in mind, is your handshake "interview-ready?"

I've had the most amazingly burly men offer me handshakes that were so "wimpy" they completely destroyed my impression of their initial personal brand image. No matter how you look, if you don't offer a handshake that comes across as confident, you run the risk of hurting your personal brand.

On the other hand, is your handshake just the opposite of wimpy? I've had some people crush my hand so badly with a forceful handshake that my ring engraved itself into my finger in a matter of seconds. What kind of personal brand message do you think that individual just communicated to me? A bully? Someone who must have their way by force? In either case, it's someone I would never want to work with!

I don't know of any schools that offer a "Handshake 101" course, so unfortunately, most of us are never taught the best way to shake hands. It's key to practice your handshake if you aren't sure about it. It should be firm and link thumb-to-thumb with the other person. If you're afraid of being too forceful or not sure if you're squeezing too hard, ask someone you trust to let you shake their hand. Then, ask them to tell you honestly what kind of signal your handshake is communicating.

Also, if you have a tendency to get sweaty palms, keep a handkerchief or tissue in your pocket to wipe your hands right before the interview. Maybe you have poor circulation, and your hands are always cold? If so, place your hand in your pocket to warm it up before you go into an interview, or go to the nearest restroom and run warm water over your hands. Whatever you do, make sure your handshake is communicating your personal brand effectively, or it could put you at a disadvantage from the very start of your interview.

Don't Forget to Breathe! Let's be honest: Interviews can be nerve-wracking experiences, and it's a medical fact that when you're nervous, your breathing is likely to become shallower. The solution? Take subtle deep breaths to help calm you down. You don't want it to be obvious that you're breathing deeply, but it's important to make sure you don't hold your breath or breathe shallowly and rapidly due to nervousness. The last thing you want is not to get enough oxygen to your brain where you've stored all those great answers to potential interview questions! If you find that your breathing is not deep enough due to nerves, pause for a second, and take a subtle but deep breath.

If you tend to have excess nervous energy in interviews, practice calming yourself before you walk into the interviewer's office. Do some deep breathing to get your heart rate down, and keep your hands clasped together on your lap if they tend to fidget. Concentrate on keeping your feet flat on the floor, and turn your attention to what the interviewer is saying to ease your anxiety.

Watch Out for Nervous Body Language. You may have adopted habits that go against the brand you want to communicate. Say, for example, you're in an interview, and you suddenly hear an annoying tapping sound. Look around—it might be you tapping your foot or a pen against a table! Just like a leg that bounces up and down uncontrollably, most people are completely unaware of the unconscious signals they send to others simply by how they move. If you exhibit nervous Actions that you're not even aware of, begin to notice them to gain control of your excitement. The body language you communicate may actually come across to your interviewer as a lack of self-confidence.

Do you:

- Bite your nails?
- Drum your fingers?
- Swing your leg?
- Blink rapidly?
- Grip the arms of your chair?

These are all Actions that will make you appear anxious. Here are some additional typical nervous body language habits to watch out for:

- Avoid fidgeting. Stay as still as you can (without becoming rigid, of course), or you may risk coming across as impatient.
- Try not to use your hands more than necessary when you speak. According to psychologists who have studied body language, confident people don't feel the need to prove their points by gesturing too much.
- Don't let your eyes wander while the interviewer is speaking. If your eyes *do* wander, the interviewer may get the idea that you're not interested in what he or she is saying, which may give the impression that you're not very interested in the job!

Maintain "Open" Body Language. In interview situations, good personal brand builders practice body language that makes them appear "open" and friendly. Here are some "open" body language tips:

- Avoid folding your arms across your chest because it communicates that you're closing yourself off to other people.
- Avoid putting your hands in your pockets during the interview because it can be interpreted as protectiveness.
- If you want your interviewer to know you're interested in what he or she is saying, lean forward slightly.
- If you want to show sincerity when making a point, touch your palm to your chest as you speak.

- Men, when you first walk into an interview, have your suit jacket buttoned, but feel free to unbutton it when you sit down. Not only will this keep your jacket from bunching up, but it will communicate YOU™ as someone who is receptive.

- What about when you're sitting? Experts say it's fine to cross your legs.

- Don't lean back in your chair, however, or clasp your hands behind your head. This conveys an attitude that's too casual and may even come across as *over*-confident, making you potentially less likeable to an interviewer.

- If you're sitting at a table, resting your elbows on the table with the fingertips of both your hands touching is considered an expression of self-confidence.

Observe the body language of people you feel drawn to. What are they doing that makes them so likeable? On the other hand, what Actions do you see in people who are not that likeable or approachable? Once again, this is why videotaping yourself prior to interviews can be so valuable. You may notice yourself unconsciously doing something that you've seen unapproachable people do. By discovering it now, you can fix it before it derails you in an interview.

Take Notes. Taking a few notes while in the interviewer's office communicates a conscientious personal brand and has the added benefit of helping you to remember key points of the interview later on as well. You don't want to be seen as writing down every single word that is said, but, for example, when you ask questions about the company, it's perfectly fine to write down a few brief notes. Be sure to write down names and titles of key people who are mentioned during your interview. You will definitely use those later, and your personal brand will be received positively as a result.

Leave the Interviewer Impressed with YOU™. When you walk out of an interview, make sure you leave a lasting impression. Stand up, offer your goodbye handshake, look the interviewer respectfully in the eye, and smile. We'll talk later about what to say when you're leaving, but your Actions — your body language — at the end of an interview will play a key role in what the interviewer remembers about you long after you have left.

Your Actions *After* the Interview

Strong personal brand builders know that they must keep up with their Actions as much *after* interviews as before and during interviews. That's key to communicating a job-seeker personal brand properly. Here are some tips for after an interview is over.

Summarize Immediately. As soon as an interview is finished, find a quiet place to sit down, and write your summary of the meeting. Don't expect that you'll remember enough to write it later. You will inevitably forget some important points even if you wait just an hour or two after the interview. Trust me — after several meetings with a number of companies, the interviews will start to blend together in your mind unless you take good notes right away. When your job search is in full swing, you'll be glad you made the time to summarize immediately.

As you think back and jot down notes, ask yourself: What were the key topics you and the interviewer discussed? What were the names of the critical decision makers who were mentioned? What did you notice about the company environment? Were you treated well? Did you get a "good feeling" while you were there? Writing down notes after the interview will help you refer to important points in follow-up e-mails and also refresh your memory when it comes time for a second interview. Believe me — remembering your first interview well will communicate a great "conscientious" personal brand, and you can't go wrong with that kind of brand image.

Follow Up. Don't take it personally if you don't hear back quickly from your interviewer. Managers are often so busy that, even though the hiring process is extremely important, they are sometimes forced to put it on the back burner. In fact, some companies have fairly complex processes to follow before anyone can be hired, including asking other employees for input. So, don't sweat it if you don't hear back right away.

All that said, you should definitely follow up immediately with a thank you e-mail. We'll address this more in the Sound chapter, but this is a critical Action that will help you stand out from the crowd. Write the thank you within 24 hours after your interview at the latest. The interviewer may be conducting one interview after another, so get that thank you to him or her while YOU™ are still fresh in the interviewer's mind!

Haven't heard back from your interviewer, and it's been about a week or more since your interview? It's okay to call and leave a voicemail message or send a follow-up e-mail to let the interviewer know you're still interested. The key is to ask the question politely, and just let him or her know that you're still interested in working for the company. If you have a chance to actually get someone on the phone, you can mention something about the interview that you've been thinking about and, once again, how well you believe your background and experience would fit with the job.

If you've been told, for example, that the decision will be made about the job within two weeks of your interview, send a follow-up e-mail a few days before that deadline. If you still hear nothing from the interviewer, perhaps follow up in another week or two, depending on how quickly the interviewer indicated the job would be filled. After two or three follow-ups, you can probably assume that you didn't get the job if you don't hear anything from the interviewer.

A Second Interview. If you're called for a second or third interview, don't change your strategy, but keep building on it! You've made it this far because of who YOU™ are, so keep doing what you did in the first interview by keeping your Audience and their Needs top of mind. And don't forget you are communicating your job-seeker personal brand every moment. In second or third interviews, for example, you might be taken for a walking tour around the company. If this happens, remember that your Actions, Reactions, Look, Sound, and Thoughts will all be observed even during this less formal time.

Your Job-Seeker Personal Brand Marketing Plan

Reflecting on all of the Actions outlined in this chapter, which ones do you think you should work on most or improve as you consider how to effectively communicate your job-seeker personal brand? With those in mind, it's time to pull together your Job-Seeker Personal Brand Marketing Plan. To help you, Jamie and Marcia have completed their Actions Job-Seeker Personal Brand Marketing Plans. Review their Marketing Plans, and complete your own for your Actions. What will YOU™ do to communicate your personal brand through your Actions?

Jamie's
Job-Seeker
Personal Brand
Summary:

Actions

A "Finish Line Champion" who supervises, trains, and motivates the team through a creative collaborative process to meet or beat customer deadlines.

Videotape myself in a mock interview. Work on eliminating nervous body language; particularly stop the bad habit of tapping my pen on tables.

Marcia's
Job-Seeker
Personal Brand
Summary:

Actions

"Experienced, Trusted Communicator" who uses good judgment to make sure work is done efficiently and accurately and who always communicates fully with the VP of Finance.

After first interview experience, practice storytelling and sharing examples from the past that illustrate self-management, trustworthiness, and ability to make strong decisions. Work on strengthening handshake.

Now that you've seen how Jamie and Marcia will use their Actions to market their personal brands, you should have an idea of what Actions you can take to communicate YOU™. What Actions do you need to work on in order to make your personal brand a reality in the minds of your Audience?

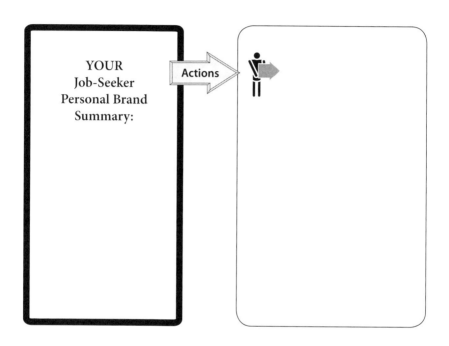

Strong personal brand builders know that
they must keep up with their Actions
before, during, and after *interviews.*

Communicate it

Reactions

Step 2

13

Reactions

Job-Seeker Personal Brand Marketing Plan Activity #2

It's not the situation. It's your reaction to the situation.
— Robert Conklin, Author

Remember when former U.S. President Bill Clinton was proven to have lied under oath? When he was accused of sexual misconduct in the White House, at first he vehemently denied what was later proven to be true. A few years after that, when President Clinton published his memoir, he addressed the situation quite differently and told the truth, explaining it as a mistake. So, his first Reaction when faced with a tough challenge was to lie. His second Reaction was to explain it as a personal failure. Ultimately, he recovered well from the entire affair (every pun intended!), but it's a great lesson in how important Reactions can be and the kind of impact your Reactions can have on your personal brand.

Most of us face our biggest personal brand Reaction challenges when we're nervous or under the gun. If you want to see someone's true personal brand emerge, watch them react to a difficult situation. Does that sound like an interview to you? A tough interview environment can cause self-control to fall apart, and — if you're not careful — all the work you've done to communicate your personal brand can be erased in one fell swoop. Let's face it: When things are going great, it's easy to stay consistent with your personal brand. It's when you're nervous and things *aren't* going very well that you find it hard to maintain the personal brand you want to communicate.

Maybe you're one of the lucky few who don't see an interview as a challenging situation, but most people in job search mode find that interviews are sometimes stressful enough to cause them to lose control of their Reactions. How you react to events and circumstances in job search situations can make or break your job-seeker personal brand. If something happens in the interview that causes you to have a negative knee-jerk Reaction, you could seriously undermine your brand, preventing you from landing the job you really want.

The Reactions I'm talking about here are Reactions you can see, read, or hear—how YOU™ might respond to an unexpected challenge or perhaps to an interviewer's Actions. (Your Reactions can also take the form of negative Thought Reactions, but that's not the focus of this particular chapter. We'll get to that subject later on.) The Reactions YOU™ make—that can be seen, read, or heard—will definitely influence the way potential employers perceive, think, and feel about you as an applicant.

The bottom line is this: The way you react will serve as a real "torture test" for sticking to and communicating your personal brand, especially in interviews and throughout the entire process of searching for a job.

Whose Emotions Are These Anyway?

Have you ever heard the phrase, "You can't always control what happens to you, but you can control how you react to it?" I'm not sure who originally coined this phrase, but I couldn't agree more. We often say, "He made me feel bad about my resume," or "Her comments about my cover letter made me so angry!" The truth is that someone else's Actions may push a button that leads to your emotions, but only *you* are responsible for how you react. No one can "make" you feel anything. You are in charge, so you can actually take over and learn to transform your Reactions into something else. It's really about mastering self-control.

Think about how you might typically react to something unexpected or unpleasant that happens to you. Maybe you found out about a change of appointment time two minutes before you were leaving for an interview, or an interviewer made a snide remark about something on your resume. If you're like most people, your automatic Reaction probably comes instinctually—from your "gut"—without any conscious thought.

An automatic Reaction like that may simply be based on a habit you've developed over time. Sometimes, without even realizing it, a comment someone makes can bring up a negative situation from years ago and send you into emotional overdrive. Or maybe you've conditioned yourself to react in a certain way because that's the way you saw your parents respond when bad things happened. You might have had a boss for a long time who went on a tirade if you didn't respond immediately to a question or an incident. So, your negative Reactions may just be bad habits in disguise.

Taking Control

Learning to get rid of old Reaction habits and replacing them with new, more positive habits can be difficult. In fact, learning to control your emotions is generally a lifetime lesson. But the truth is that knee-jerk Reactions almost always lead to conflict, and they probably won't help you get the job you want. In other words, knee-jerk Reactions during your job search will most probably just make things worse for you in the long run.

Here's an example: Rob was a public relations specialist, and he had a job interview coming up at one of his top targeted companies that he was really nervous about. He had left his last job because he didn't get along well with his boss. In fact, the situation at his job had gone from bad to worse until he and his former boss ended up in a shouting match, and Rob got fired. He felt in his own mind that he and his boss just had a personality clash but — no matter the cause — the outcome meant he couldn't list his former boss as a reference. Needless to say, it made Rob's job search tougher because he knew he would have to explain the situation in every single interview.

For this particular interview at the company where Rob really wanted a job, he entered the interviewer's office as always, prepared with his answers to the difficult questions he expected would be asked. The interviewer probed very deeply about Rob's past boss and asked more and more questions about the situation. What specifically about his supervisor didn't Rob like? What was it about Rob that his supervisor didn't like? Does Rob find it hard to get along with people? How could he be sure something like this wouldn't happen again? Why should the new employer take a chance on him? These were all fair questions, and they were questions Rob had prepared for in advance. But what he wasn't quite prepared for was an interviewer who was very suspicious and spoke in what Rob felt was an accusatory tone.

As a result, Rob fell victim to a knee-jerk Reaction, and he became defensive. He didn't completely lose his cool, but he definitely didn't respond with the kind of calm that he knew would have communicated true confidence. Instead, he let himself get rattled by the interviewer and ended up blaming the situation entirely on his former supervisor, sounding defensive in the end. Needless to say, Rob didn't get the job.

Avoid Regrets

If you're like me, you can think of incidents you wish you could relive, reacting in a different way that wouldn't make you cringe later. One way to gain better control over your Reactions is to think about how you want to remember interview experiences in the future. You don't want to have regrets, right? How could you react in a way that you would be proud to remember later?

Do remember, too, that time heals. Can you recall an incident that happened to you when you were younger that you thought you'd never recover from? Maybe you even had a terrible interview experience where you reacted in a way that haunted you for a long time. We all have experiences like this, and most of the time, they're not as bad when we think back on them as they were at the time we experienced them.

When I'm on the verge of reacting negatively, I've found it helpful to take a moment and ask myself: "Is this really as bad as I think it is?" Once the initial flood of emotion passes, I can better separate my emotions from the situation and see things more clearly. So, overreacting will most likely just lead to a regretful memory, especially if it seriously undermines your personal brand during the job search process. Why add to your list of unpleasant memories?

Just as we mentioned in the Actions chapter, your Reactions can affect your job search before, during, and after your interviews. So, what can you do to make sure your Reactions promote and support your job-seeker personal brand throughout your job search?

Your Reactions *Before* the Interview

It's important to be ready with your Reactions before a tough interview situation comes up. But how do you do that?

Be Prepared. As we said in the Actions chapter, you'll want to have an answer ready for every question you can think of that might come up in an interview. And, if you're like Rob, and you have something in your work history that might be hard to talk about with an interviewer, be sure to prepare your answers carefully in advance, keeping in mind what your typical Reactions might be to a negative question. For example, let's say an interviewer challenges you about your history of frequently changing jobs. You could say, "Actually, that variety of experiences helped me to get clear about the kind of job I really want, and that's why I'm here today." Or, perhaps you could acknowledge a weakness that you have by saying, "Yes, that is definitely something I've been actively working to improve." Then, go on to explain to the interviewer what you're doing to strengthen that weakness. (Don't forget about Appendix A, the list of great questions to be ready to answer and to ask in an interview.)

How Would YOU™ React? Keep your job-seeker personal brand summary in mind, and think about how someone with that brand would respond during an interview. Consider many different scenarios and desired Reactions based on how you want an interviewer to see YOU™. This exercise can serve as a great "tool chest" for dealing with a whole range of possibilities that could come up in a job interview.

By doing this, you'll be able to move beyond your "gut" Reaction to a place where you can just automatically think: "This is the type of situation where someone with my job-seeker personal brand would respond by focusing on my Unique Strengths instead of what's going wrong." Working through an entire range of possible personal brand Reactions will give you confidence that you know how to react when something unexpected comes your way.

Facial Reactions. Do you wear your heart on your sleeve ... or, rather, your face? If you're someone who tends to be transparent — baring your feelings and thoughts on your face for all to see — try practicing your "poker face" in the mirror before your interviews. The more you practice, the better you will be able to keep your cool when you're sitting across from an interviewer. Ask some close friends to help you practice by having them say unexpected and upsetting things to you. Then, see how calm you can keep your face without reflecting what you're really thinking and feeling.

It's key, of course, that you actually believe what they're saying, so you should really imagine that it's an interviewer saying these things to you. Be the actor, and make the situation real for yourself. Then, you can bring on the emotions you might actually experience during an interview. With practice, it will become very natural for you to show only the emotions you really want others to see. You'll be able to put it to use during your job search and even later, on the job, if you need it.

Telephone and E-mail. Never respond on the phone or in an e-mail in a way that you wouldn't respond if you were face-to-face. If a secretary or receptionist is rude to you on the phone or in an e-mail, don't react negatively! Take a deep breath and count to five in your head — whatever it takes. While this person may not be the interviewer or your potential boss, he or she could easily make negative remarks about you to the person with the hiring power. It simply isn't worth it to have a knee-jerk response to someone who may just be having a bad day. Remember the personal brand you're working to communicate, and pick your battles. The satisfaction of telling someone off for a petty comment is much less than the satisfaction of getting a great position in a terrific company.

Your Reactions *During* the Interview

Of course, your Reactions during the interview are of primary importance, but it's key when you're face-to-face with an interviewer to focus on more than just controlling your nerves. Why? Well, the Reactions we're talking about are ones your interviewer can plainly see or hear. So, there are a few things to pay particular attention to when "it's showtime!"

Too Dry? If you tend to suffer from dry mouth when you get nervous and need to speak, carry a small bottle of water with you. It's better to do that than to find it hard to get your words out during an interview because your lips are parched.

Verbal Control. Do you tend to become easily angry or defensive in the face of an unexpected situation? If so, it's important to take a breath before responding, and give yourself a moment to calm down. In fact, sometimes, the less said, the better. Indeed, the best Reaction to this kind of unexpected situation might just be to remain quiet. The absence of a verbal Reaction can actually communicate strength and conviction. So, learn to be comfortable with silence when it's appropriate, and it might actually work to your benefit.

Speaking of Silence

Some interviewers have been known to stay quiet for several seconds just to see how the interviewee will handle it. If an interviewer becomes quiet for an unusually long time, wait a moment, then ask if he or she would like to have any further clarification about the last question asked.

But don't feel you have to rush to fill the silence with just anything that comes to mind. This is the kind of Reaction that might cause you to babble or accidentally share something that could be perceived as negative about yourself. In some cases, your interviewer may just be having a bad day and struggling to stay focused. So, just naturally continue the conversation by asking what else he or she would like to know about you or by asking questions about the company and/or the position.

Take Your Time. When asked a question by the interviewer, rather than burst out with any response that pops into your head, take a few seconds to think about what you want to say before you answer. If you're really stumped about how to respond, you might even say, "That's a good question; let me take a moment to think about that." It shows that you're really putting thought into your responses. It's better to have a few seconds of silence to gather your thoughts than to rush and stumble on your words (which, let's face it, we often do when we're nervous).

Creative Reactions Under Pressure. Let's say you've been asked to share a story from your past to show how you handled a particular type of tough situation. Your brain races through a dozen options, but you're coming up empty for examples from your work life. Don't fret! If you can't find any example from your past work experience, think of how you solved a similar type of problem at home or in some other context. Don't force a square peg into a round hole, of course, but feel free to ask the interviewer if it's okay to share an example from an area of your life other than work. Obviously, you would only do this when the example really does apply to the question at hand,

and you'll want to make sure the story isn't too personal. But this tactic is a great example of a creative Reaction under pressure.

Don't Fake It! If you truly don't know the answer to a question, absolutely avoid making something up. How's that going to help the "authentic" YOU™? Tell the interviewer you're not sure of the answer, and volunteer to find out so that you can call the interviewer back as soon as possible with a response. Explain that you'd rather do the research to find out more than to answer in a way that might be misleading. Most interviewers won't see this as a negative; they may even see it as a sign of integrity.

Another caution about "faking it" is to pretend you understand a question when you really don't. You shouldn't feel badly about asking the interviewer to repeat or clarify a particular question. You might think you'll look "stupid" by doing so, but the truth is you'll only look stupid if you answer the question in a way that doesn't make sense.

React to Your Reactions. If your nerves cause you to get a bit tongue-tied during an interview, don't be afraid to acknowledge it, make a joke, and move on. You could simply say something like, "Wow! I guess my nerves got the better of me there for a moment!" There's nothing wrong with being honest about feeling some nervousness in an interview situation — everyone does. As long as your nerves don't prevent you from effectively communicating your job-seeker personal brand, a small acknowledgement here or there won't do YOU™ any serious damage.

Your Reactions *After* the Interview

Write It Down. As mentioned in the Actions chapter, immediately after the interview — while the experience is fresh — find a quiet space and "unload your mind," writing down all you can remember from the interview. Just write and write and write. Don't think about how well the interview went until you have all of your memories down on paper. Then, and only then, ask yourself: How effectively did I manage my Reactions? How well did I answer any difficult questions? Did I keep my cool? What Reactions can I work on improving for my next interview? This is how you continue to improve your Reactions over time.

Use Every Experience to Improve. If things didn't go exactly as you planned, don't be too hard on yourself. Just focus on what you did well and what you can improve on in the future. Remember: No one is perfect. The key is to learn from your mistakes, figure out what you would do better the next time, and add it to your Marketing Plan as something to work on.

Don't Let a Rejection Get You Down. If you get a "no" response after an interview, that's okay. In fact, look at it as a way to save you time and money. Why? Because you can now focus on other target companies or jobs where you have more potential. Nora Bammann of The Kroger Company says: "Rejections are tough but (a) you got interview practice, and (b) you can use the experience to further refine your job search criteria."

When a "no" happens, take the time to evaluate what you would have liked the most about that position and what you would have liked the least. You can then use this information as you continue to hone in on the best companies and jobs for YOU™. It can also help you to come up with better questions to ask in future interviews. Think about what retired professional basketball player Michael Jordan said: "I've missed over 9,000 shots in my career. I've lost almost 300 games. Twenty-six times, I've been trusted to take the game-winning shot ... and missed. I've failed over and over and over again in my life. And that is why I succeed." The truth is that we learn the most, and uncover what we need to improve upon, primarily through failing.

A "No" Can Still Be a Connection. Don't throw away any of the information about your interviewer! You never know what can happen from the connections you make during an interview. You may be called in for a different job with that same company at a later date, or the interviewer may get a new position elsewhere and remember you.

Here's a personal example of how important this is: When I was looking for my very first job right out of college, I interviewed with a company that was offering a position I really wanted. After a couple of (what I thought were good) interviews, I was told the crushing news: I didn't get the job. I was incredibly disappointed, but I resigned myself to the bad news and wrote a thank you note anyway to the person who would have been my boss. In the note,

I said I was very interested in the company and that I'd like to be considered for any future openings. One month later, the person who had just been hired for that original job was fired. One phone call and one more interview later, I got the job. I learned firsthand that a "no" doesn't have to be forever. So, hold on to your interviewers' information — you never know when it might come in handy again.

Ask for Feedback. If you receive a "no," use it as an opportunity to learn how you could increase your chances the next time. If you feel comfortable with it, ask your interviewer politely if he or she would be willing to share a reason or two why you were turned down. You can explain, of course, that this will help you to improve in your next interview. You might ask if there was anything in particular from your interview or perhaps something about your background or experience that drove the decision. Would they consider you for any other jobs where your qualifications might be appropriate? This is a great example of how you can succeed by failing — just like Michael Jordan.

Don't Relax Too Much in a Second Interview. If you get called back for a second or third interview, it's easy to get lulled into believing you're just a signature away from "You're hired!" But this can be dangerous. Most HR experts agree that it's actually in follow-up interviews that a large number of candidates fall out of the hiring pool. Remember: Be watchful about communicating your job-seeker personal brand in *every* interview, not just the first or second one. Once you have the formal hiring letter and you've signed it and sent it in, consider yourself hired; until then, it's key to keep a steady course and never stop communicating YOU™.

Putting Your Reactions into Action

Now, let's check in on Jamie and Marcia to see what Reaction plans they will use in their Job-Seeker Personal Brand Marketing Plans.

Jamie's
Job-Seeker
Personal Brand
Summary:

A *"Finish Line Champion"* who supervises, trains, and motivates the team through a creative collaborative process to meet or beat customer deadlines.

Reactions

Speak with the recruiter that was recommended and come up with a list of potential questions I might be asked; then, practice answering and get feedback from the recruiter.

Marcia's
Job-Seeker
Personal Brand
Summary:

"Experienced, Trusted Communicator" who uses good judgment to make sure work is done efficiently and accurately and who always communicates fully with the VP of Finance.

Reactions

Practice "poker face" in response to challenging questions.

What Reactions do you need to work on to make your job-seeker personal brand more powerful?

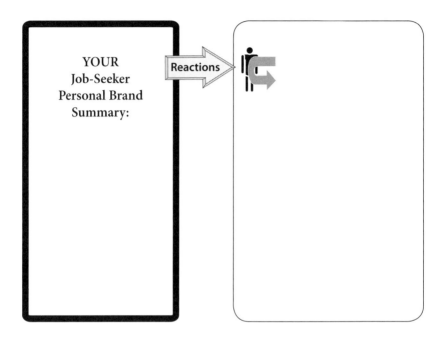

" Most of us face our biggest personal brand Reaction challenges when we're nervous or under the gun. "

"Your resume is outstanding, but somehow we don't feel you're quite right for this firm!"

Communicate it

Look

14

Look

Job-Seeker Personal Brand Marketing Plan Activity #3

Never trust a skinny chef.

— Anonymous

If there is ever a time when first impressions matter, it's in a job interview. Study after study tells us that interviewers form an opinion about a candidate as quickly as 15 to 20 seconds after the start of the interview. Since there clearly hasn't been much said in that short time, the cold, hard reality is: The opinion the interviewer has about you has been based primarily on how you look.

I can hear you out there saying, "Give me a break! I wasn't born with a movie star face or body ... what can I do about that?" Hey, I'm no beauty queen myself, and no one expects you to be either. It's not about being gorgeous; it's about presenting the best possible Look for the job-seeker personal brand you want to communicate.

You've probably heard the old adage: "You never get a second chance to make a first impression." Unfortunately, it really is true. Now, that doesn't mean you won't necessarily get a chance to make a *second* impression that could change the first impression someone has of you. But no matter how you slice it, that first image is a tough one to undo. It takes hard work to make someone change their first impression of you since that first personal brand image happens so quickly — and unconsciously. Creating the best Look for your job-seeker personal brand will help you come across as the YOU™ that you want your Audience to see.

The Packaged YOU™

Think of your Look as your "packaging." Just like a bottle that holds shampoo has been designed with a certain brand image in mind, so your Look — your own "packaging" — communicates a whole host of things about you, too. Just from your Look, potential employers will form opinions about your values, your attitudes, your worth, who you are, what you stand for, and what you have to offer.

Big companies put a lot of time and money into developing a brand's package design because they know how important the "outside" is to an overall brand image. They know that a brand's Character comes through loud and clear through a brand's packaging, and they know that Character has a lot to do with how well that brand actually sells.

If you think about it, doesn't packaging help you make brand choices when you're shopping? Imagine yourself standing in a supermarket aisle, and you have to choose between two brands you don't know much about. All other things being equal, if you're like most people, you're probably going to choose the brand with the packaging you like the best.

Guess what? Potential employers look at the trademarked YOU™ the same way.

Listen, I know you can't control every aspect of your Look. And I'm definitely not suggesting you head for a plastic surgeon's office! But what's key is simply to take charge of those aspects of your Look that *are* in your control. In the job search process, this means paying attention to things like the "Look" of your cover letter, the quality of your clothing, how well you're groomed, etc. Remember: You really are the Brand Manager of YOU™, and it's your job to make sure your packaging sets you up for a great impression at first glance.

Watch Out!

If you're like a lot of folks, you may have always thought that personal branding is mostly about how you Look — your hair style, how you dress, whether or not you're wearing the "right" tie or length of skirt, etc. But smart personal branding is definitely not just about wearing the right suit. Trying to communicate a great personal brand simply by wearing the right clothing or by only thinking about how you look is just scratching the surface of who YOU™ really are … and it definitely isn't enough to land you the job you really want.

Don't get me wrong — your Look is absolutely important to your personal brand! There's no question that Look plays a big part in helping to communicate YOU™. (I wouldn't have devoted an entire chapter to it if it didn't!) But all that said, you know by now that your personal brand is made up of so much more than just the way you look.

Your Look *Before* the Interview

Your Look is not just about trying to be beautiful or handsome. It's about transmitting your personal brand in the world. It's about "embodying" the brand that YOU™ want to get across.

So, how should you look and what should you wear as you're planning for an interview? It depends. If you're being interviewed for a creative job (like a graphic designer position or a writer), feel free to let loose a bit more. Use your best judgment based on what you've learned about the company. Have you found out what people usually wear at the office? Use what you know about the current employees' dress, but bear in mind that while business casual may be fine for every day at the office, it's best to dress a bit more formally in an interview. Lastly, of course, you want to take into account the job-seeker personal brand you're communicating. Make your Look a great combination of who YOU™ are and what your Audience is looking for.

Here are some general guidelines that have been proven to work for your Look when it comes to job interviews.

Your Cover Letter and Resume. Before potential interviewers ever lay eyes on you, they have already had an experience of your "Look" through your cover letter and resume. These few pieces of paper or e-mailed documents are absolutely an advertisement for YOU™, so it's your opportunity to make a strong first impression before your interviewer even sees you face-to-face.

Make sure your letter and resume are not only written well, but that they *look* attractive. Are they laid out well so that the important information is easy to find? If they are printed, use white or off-white paper. If they're digital, make sure to use a white background with black print and a font that's easy to read. Unless you're applying for a job as a graphic designer or artist, avoid anything fancy to stand out from the crowd, which includes avoiding emoticons in professional e-mails. According to Liz Handlin, CEO of Ultimate-Resumes.com, "Unless you're looking for a job that values creativity above all else, you will risk coming across unprofessional if you use cute stationery, colored fonts, or smiley faces."

Your Hair. Unless you're interviewing for a rock band, keep this in mind: Spikes belong on the bottom of golf shoes, not in your hair during an interview! Not to sound too stodgy, but honestly, for an interview, you're better off keeping your hair simple and well-groomed … no matter how little or how much hair you have to work with. Your best bet is to communicate a solid job-seeker personal brand by aiming for a hairstyle that most people would simply consider "neat and professional."

Your Skin. You may be thinking, "My skin? What the heck does my skin have to do with my personal brand? Interviewers don't care about that, too, do they?" Well, let's face it: Your skin is one of the most visible parts of your physical appearance, and it can actually say a lot about how well you take care of yourself. I can hear you saying, "Unfair! I wasn't blessed with flawless skin." Well, join the sizable club — most of us weren't. You don't have to have perfect skin; you just need to do the best with what you have. Simply learn what your skin needs in order to look as healthy as possible … and this goes for men, too.

For the Men. Let's face it, guys: In recent times, dozens of new male skin care products have been introduced into the market for a reason. More and more attention is being paid to how well men take care of themselves. So, gentlemen, the (skincare) bar is rising. Step up to the plate, and check out a product or two. This means shaving daily — sorry! — and carefully (assuming your personal brand isn't Colin-Farrell-tough-boy, of course).

For the Women. When men get older, they somehow look more "sophisticated," but when women age, they sometimes find themselves relegated to the back office. How's that for a harsh reality? It's an unfair truth that men seem to be able to get away with much more during the aging process. It is what it is … for now. So, women, just accept that looking young requires a bit more work. Great personal brand builders do!

Here's another startling reality: Women who wear makeup earn 20% to 30% more money than those who don't. I strongly recommend that all women ignore this advice — unless, of course, you want to make more money! If you don't like to wear makeup, that's fine — just keep it light and simple. Too much is worse than too little, but too little will do nothing to help your job-seeker personal brand (or your pocketbook).

Lastly, if you haven't yet heard about the damage that UV rays do to your skin, what rock have you been living under!? All kidding aside, those nasty statistics are true. I've had family members who have suffered with serious skin cancers, so this is no laughing matter. Even if your personal brand is about being rugged, too much time in the sun will eventually catch up with you and can result in skin cancer. Nothing is worth that.

Your Body. Another tried-but-true piece of advice is to get regular exercise. How many times have you heard this one? But many medical studies have proven this to be right: Exercise makes you look better because it makes you healthier. Here's what else exercise has been proven to help you do:

- Makes you feel better.
- Helps your clothes fit better.
- Increases your blood circulation, which improves the color of your skin.
- Makes you sleep better, which reduces dark eye circles and eye bags.

Hard to refute all of that, isn't it? So, get out there and exercise. The healthier you look, the more employers will want you to be part of their team. With that in mind, doesn't your job-seeker personal brand deserve a jog around the park?

Your Clothes. The trend in some developed countries during the last decade and a half has been toward casual wear in offices. Yet, a *USA Today* article I read a while back revealed that, during this time, sexual harassment lawsuits in corporate America have skyrocketed. "Why?" the article asked. The hypothesis is that people are dressing so casually in the office — the same way they might be dressed in a bar, for example — that their behavior in the office begins to mimic their behavior in bars. So, how we dress sends signals to ourselves and those around us about what is and isn't proper behavior. Don't underestimate the importance of that!

The bottom line is: Unless you're applying for a job as a fashion designer, you want to be remembered for your skills, not your clothes. You want the interviewer to focus on you, not what you're wearing. So, make sure your clothes are good quality, but avoid bright colors. Whether you like it or not, more conservative blacks, grays, and navy blues work best in most interview situations. In general, if you go with one of those colors, you can't go wrong.

Actors will often tell you that they can immediately step into character when they're given the right costume. So, how you dress not only influences the way others perceive you, but it will probably impact how you perceive yourself as well and, therefore, how you act. And you already know how important your Actions are when it comes to communicating your job-seeker personal brand in an interview.

Think of it this way: If you want to "act" professionally, you need to wear the right costume for the play you're in. As a smart personal brand builder, you want to make sure everything you wear communicates your brand and says what YOU™ want to say during your all-important job search.

So, dress for success — literally — as if you're going to meet the most important V.I.P. of your life. For most jobs, an interview isn't a place where casual dress is likely to work, no matter what you may have heard about the dress code of that company. Unless the interviewer specifically instructs you to dress casually, play it smart, and don't take chances.

Here are some other things to consider when choosing a wardrobe for YOU™:

- Invest in *quality* clothes. Spend less time worrying about the latest fashion, which is often too over-the-top for anything but the fashion industry anyway. Even if your budget isn't quite at a point where you can have a full wardrobe that's just perfect for the personal brand you want to communicate, spend the extra time and money to get some good quality items. People tend to pay more attention to quality than quantity anyway.

- Make sure your clothes are clean — not worn, torn, or missing buttons. Here is a personal story related to this: When I managed laundry brands at Procter & Gamble, all I had to do was say I worked in detergents, and everyone inevitably looked immediately at … you guessed it … my clothes. Remember our skinny chef from the opening quote of this chapter? It was the same thing. People I met expected that my clothes would be in tip-top shape because of my job. Talk about pressure! So, I started paying more attention to what I was wearing to make sure my clothing would pass a spot inspection. It actually turned out to be a good lesson in personal brand building. My clothes and I represented the Cheer and Ariel brands back then just as you represent the YOU™ brand in your interviews. You owe it to your personal brand — and to your job search — to do YOU™ justice with the clothes you wear.

- Spend some time to look at your clothes objectively from an outsider's perspective. This is especially true for clothes you wear to interviews. What does your wardrobe say about YOU™? If you find it hard to be objective, ask a trusted friend or even an image consultant to give you an opinion. Then, be sure to check and recheck your interview clothes for frayed hems, rips, stains, and hanging threads. Do you have a skirt or jacket that is well past its wear-out date? If so, wouldn't you feel better letting those items go? Do it for YOU™!

Your Accessories. When it comes to accessories, there are two key principles that great personal branders follow: First, aim for quality, not quantity. Choose your accessories carefully, and don't overdo it. Accessories (belts, ties, cufflinks, scarves, and jewelry) are just that — accessories. That means they're supposed to add to what you're wearing — not overpower your Look.

Second, check to see that your accessories are consistent with what YOU™ want to stand for and what your Audience will find appropriate. If your brand is "reliable with the occasional surprising edge," then, by all means go ahead and clip a funny pin on your jacket lapel, or wear a bold tie to your interview. The key is to make sure your accessories are helping to communicate your personal brand during your job search.

Your Hands. Your hands are seen in an interview a lot more than you may realize. One moment, you're using your hand to receive a company brochure from your interviewer. The next moment, you're pointing at a specific spot on your resume. The next, you're waving at an employee that you know as you leave the interviewer's office. Unless you're a factory worker, if your fingernails are ragged or dirty or your hands are dry and scaly, your hands may just be pointing to the wrong personal brand impression.

Don't underestimate the importance of having well-groomed hands — and that goes for both men and women. More and more, men are expected to have clean hands and well-groomed fingernails. If you're not already scheduling manicures as part of the proper care and feeding of your personal brand, why not start now?

Your Shoes. I've heard it said your shoes reveal the true you, and I have to admit: When I was single, a man's shoes were often one of the first things I noticed. Were his shoes clean? Scuffed? Shined? Out of style? Cheap? I promise you I'm not one of those people who are obsessed with shoes, but I honestly felt I could judge if a guy was right for me based on his shoes. (And, by the way, I ended up with an Allen Edmonds guy through and through.)

Shoes can and do send a strong signal about your personal brand. When you're putting together your interview outfit, stop for a second and look down. Does what you see represent your job-seeker personal brand? Take a look at the shoes in your closet, and make sure the "shoe represents YOU™."

The YOU™ Collage

Your Look and your job-seeker personal brand should go hand-in-hand, so go back and look again at your personal Brand Character statement. In that section of your Job-Seeker Personal Brand Positioning Statement, you should have five or six descriptive words or a narrative sentence that describes your Character. Keeping those words or that narrative in mind, leaf through magazines and newspapers, and cut out pictures and images that you think best visualize the image you are trying to get across. You might cut out a photo of a certain type of clothing, a well-manicured hand, a certain hairstyle, a specific pair of shoes — anything you believe conveys the look YOU™ want for your job-seeker personal brand.

Next, find some photos of you — or better yet, take photos of yourself dressed as though you're going to an interview — and place them side-by-side next to the magazine pictures you found. Compare the two. Do you see similar "branding" coming through in your own photos as compared to what you see in the magazine pictures you cut out? If not, where are you most off-track from your job-seeker personal brand image? Where are you spot-on? Where can you make adjustments? What one or two things could you change that would make the biggest difference in how YOU™ are perceived? Work on making changes to your Look until you more closely match what you liked in those magazine photos.

Your Look *During* the Interview

Now that you've taken time to prepare your Look for your interview, you should be just about ready to present the job-seeking YOU™ at your target companies. But there are a couple of other points to mention about your Look that are key to success when you're face-to-face with your interviewer.

Smile! According to facial-expression expert Paul Ekman, a Professor Emeritus of Psychology at the University of California-San Francisco, a smile can be seen from 30 meters away and immediately indicates that the person smiling has "benign intentions." So, don't be afraid to smile when you walk into an interview. In fact, smile the minute you walk into the building. If you make enough of an impression, the security guard at the building's entrance or the receptionist in the waiting area may just make a positive comment about you to a decision-maker. A natural, comfortable smile that says "I'm confident, I'm self-assured, and I'm friendly" can go miles (or at least 30 meters) to communicate the personal brand image you want.

Posture. I can still hear my mother telling me: "Watch your posture! Stand up straight!" At the time, I didn't know what a strong personal brand secret she was sharing, but now I know she was right. Great personal brand builders recognize what body language experts have said for years: Powerful self-confidence is communicated by holding your shoulders erect and not slumping. Look straight ahead as you walk, not down, especially as you enter an interviewer's office, and you will convey the kind of self-assurance that — let's face it — we all want to communicate as part of our personal brand.

The same is true when you're sitting in a chair in the interviewer's office. Don't slouch! If you're wearing a suit jacket, tuck the bottom of it underneath you as you sit down so that it doesn't bunch up around your neck.

Men, make sure your suit jacket is buttoned when you first walk into the interviewer's office, but feel free to unbutton it when you sit down. Then, button it again as you're leaving. A suit jacket looks better buttoned when you're standing, but if it's buttoned while you're sitting, it will bunch up. Women can also sometimes have this problem, so take a look at yourself in the mirror while sitting in your interview outfit.

Women, if you're planning on wearing a skirt to an interview, check to make sure it doesn't ride up too high when you sit down. How about your blouse? Does it gape open when you sit? Try it on beforehand to check yourself in a mirror. This is definitely not something you want to discover for the first time in an interviewer's office!

Don't forget about the body language that we talked about in the Actions chapter. Every one of those body language tips can impact your Look during an interview. Keep your hands in your lap, or rest your elbows on the edge of a table. Body language experts say that this conveys self-confidence. They also say that it's best for men to keep their feet flat on the floor, while it's best for women to cross their ankles under the chair.

Extensions of YOU™. Don't forget that just as your e-mails, resume, and cover letter represent the Look of your job-seeker personal brand, so does your briefcase. So, if you have an old worn-out briefcase, or if you bring important documents in a ragged manila folder with writing all over it, think about how that might look to an interviewer. You don't have to spend a lot of money on a briefcase, but make sure that you carry your resume and other materials in something neat. And keep the papers you have in your briefcase orderly as well. The last thing you want to do is open your briefcase and have a mess of disorganized papers fall out. That's not exactly the "Look" you're aiming for!

The Sweet Smell of Success. Some people don't realize that body odor is also a part of their "Look." Here are some tips to make sure YOU™ make a good "nasal" impression:

- If you have a tendency to sweat, you might want to carry a sample-size bottle of deodorant with you to an interview and apply it discreetly in the restroom after you arrive at the building where your interview will take place.

- Take breath mints with you in case you need them, and pop one in your mouth while you're sitting in the waiting room. Make sure to remove it before the interview, however, since it might get in the way of your being able to speak clearly, and chewing on a mint or gum can come across as though you're not taking the interview seriously.

- If you wear cologne or aftershave, be careful not to overdo it. You don't want your "scent" impression to be overpowering.

One Last Check. Don't forget to go into the restroom when you enter the company's office and take one last look at yourself in the mirror before the interview. Has the wind blown your hair out of place, or do you have a pen or dirt smudge on your face?

Your Look *After* the Interview

All of the same Look tips you've applied before and during your interview still apply after the interview. Stay consistent with your Look, and make sure that it always communicates the brand image you want — from the Look of your follow-up e-mails or letters to your own Look during any subsequent interviews or meetings.

Janice is an example of someone who learned the hard way the importance of being consistent when it comes to your Look. Fresh out of college, Janice was on the hunt for her first job. Within a fairly short time, she got an interview with a big bank that was at the top of her "dream company" list. That initial interview went great, and Janice was excited about the possibilities! Even so, she held her breath for two weeks while waiting to hear about a second interview.

During the time she was waiting, Janice and a friend of hers decided — on a whim — to change their hair colors. So, overnight, Janice went from a brunette to a stand-out-from-the-crowd redhead. It was a big change. Her friends loved it, but when she got invited back to her dream company for her second interview, the interviewer she had met before was, shall we say, "less than enthusiastic." In fact, when the director who interviewed Janice the first time saw her again, he was visibly startled and even made a comment about the change. It was then that Janice realized how far removed her new hair color was from the personal brand she was hoping to communicate. By making a sudden and obvious change in her appearance in between interviews, she may have been communicating a brand of "fickle" or "unstable." She didn't get the job, and it was a very hard lesson to learn about the importance of communicating her personal brand consistently.

The moral of this story is that making big, noticeable changes to the way you look during the interview process — or even changing your Look frequently after you've landed a job — may not say what you want about your willingness to be consistent in the job. Think of it from your boss's perspective. If you do something unpredictable like drastically change your hair from day to day, will you suddenly not show up for work? Will you quit your job with a week's notice in order to move to Tasmania? Okay, I'm exaggerating a bit here, but you get the point.

At work, your Audience — like all of us — has a lot of things to worry about and manage, like changes taking place in the organization, non-stop technology transformations, people moving around from job to job, and on and on. All of that change can cause stress. So, why add more change and stress to the work situation by constantly changing the way you look? It freaks people out! Like it or not — and call this stodgy if you want — people like to work with others they know they can depend on. So, you're better off not sending signals that could give a potential boss the impression that you could be "fly-by-night." Think about it: It's not your hairstyle you want to be remembered for anyway, right? It's your values, strengths, and passions that you want to come through the most in your interviews.

Just so you don't think I'm a stick-in-the-mud, if your personal brand is "raucously creative," go ahead and go for outrageous hair and occasional changes. For most of us, however, consistency in your Look is one of the best ways to communicate a consistent personal brand. This doesn't mean you shouldn't ever change your Look or your style, of course, but try to keep the changes you make more subtle while still successfully communicating your brand.

Business Casual?

Consider this scenario: You are set to have a second or third interview at a great company, and you noticed during your first interview that employees at that company dress fairly casually. Does this mean that you should also dress casually for your future interviews? Sumittra Meesuwan, Human Resources Director of MSD (Thailand) Ltd. had this to say about the subject: "The interviewee should not be casual and act as if they are already part of the company. I think the most important thing is that the interviewee should maintain their professionalism without being perceived as 'trying too hard' to blend in too quickly."

So, continue to maintain a buttoned-down professional Look until you're actually hired. It's the best way to present YOU™.

Your "Look" Marketing Plan

When you sit back and think about your personal brand image from a Look standpoint, in what ways are you doing well? Where might you be falling short? What will help your Look match the personal brand you want to communicate during your job search?

To get some different perspectives on this, let's look at how Jamie and Marcia plan to make sure their Looks are right in line with the personal brands they want to communicate in their job hunting process.

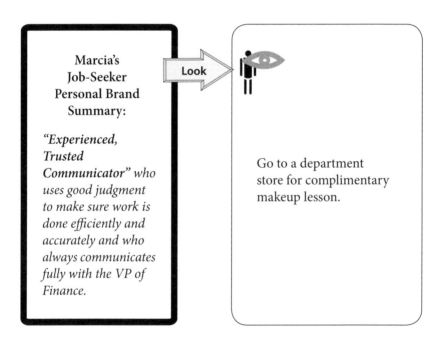

Jamie's Job-Seeker Personal Brand Summary:

A *"Finish Line Champion" who supervises, trains, and motivates the team through a creative collaborative process to meet or beat customer deadlines.*

Look

Buy a new briefcase and put together a well-organized portfolio of 3D DVD designs. Practice sitting up straight and not slouching when I sit down.

Marcia's Job-Seeker Personal Brand Summary:

"Experienced, Trusted Communicator" who uses good judgment to make sure work is done efficiently and accurately and who always communicates fully with the VP of Finance.

Look

Go to a department store for complimentary makeup lesson.

Now, think about your own job search goals. What is your Look Marketing Plan? What steps will you take to get your Look more in line with the way you want potential employers to perceive, think, and feel about YOU™?

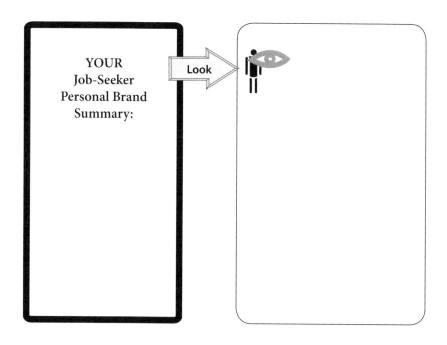

> " *Your Look is about 'embodying' the brand that YOU™ want to get across.* "

Communicate it

15

Sound

Job-Seeker Personal Brand Marketing Plan Activity #4

The greatest reward is to know that one can speak and emit articulate sounds and utter words that describe things, events, and emotions.

— Camilo Jose Cela, Spanish writer, 1989 Nobel Prize winner for literature

For our purposes, your Sound is not only what you say, but how you say it. Just like your Look, your Sound is capable of creating a split-second first impression that can make or break an interview. In fact, your Sound can even make or break your chances of getting the job during a phone call that takes place *before* a face-to-face interview.

Just how important is your Sound? Think about it: Sounds impact us often without our even realizing it. Maybe it's the sound of fingernails scraping down a blackboard, a door slamming, a strong wind howling in the middle of the night, a chime swaying in the breeze, or waves crashing onto the beach. Many sounds — not just music — absolutely have the power to influence us.

How YOU™ sound in an interview can be just as powerful and can have just as big an impact on the person who is interviewing you. Let's talk about how to control your Sound.

Are You in Control?

There are parts of your Sound that you have control over and parts of
it that are outside of your control. That's because, just like your Look,
your voice is a part of your physical self. So, even though you can change
your Sound in some ways, you can't change it completely. Let's say that,
by nature, you have a slightly nasal voice, and you've worked at it but
can only change that aspect of your Sound a bit. Well, don't let your
"Sound get you down!" Just do what you can to improve it, and keep
those changes in mind. That alone will boost your personal brand a
great deal.

The good news is: There are lots of things about your Sound that
you absolutely can — and should — work on improving to strengthen
your job-seeker personal brand.

Vary Your Pitch. While you can't change the voice you were given,
you *can* alter the pitch. An overly high or low voice can really
turn people off. I once had a secretary who was great, but her
voice — particularly on the telephone — was always at a constant,
really high pitch. It was bad enough that a few clients even
complained to me about it. I began working with her to help her
bring down her pitch. What finally worked involved my assistant
pretending that she was a big, burly man with a deep voice — very
funny considering that she was just 5 feet 2 inches tall and only
weighed 110 pounds! But, fortunately, the next thing we knew, her
voice was no longer shrill, and no more clients called to complain.
It turned out to be a lot of fun for her, too.

Before you jump into interviewing, record your voice as though
you were answering some potential interview questions. When you
play back the recording, what do you think of your pitch? Is it just
naturally high or low? If so, practice trying to move your tone up or
down. It's amazing the difference this can make. With just a little bit
of practice, you will find others listening to you more intently. That's
how you find the pitch that best communicates your job-seeker
personal brand.

If pitch turns out to be a big problem for you, and trying to change
your voice on your own proves too difficult, you might want to think
about working with a vocal coach if that's at all possible for you. It will
do your personal brand (and your self-confidence) a lot of good!

Enunciate. Another aspect of your Sound to focus on during your job search is how you enunciate words. Stating words clearly and correctly is important, no matter what personal brand you want to communicate. If you find it difficult to say words clearly, or if you sometimes stumble to pronounce words right, three things to consider are: Practice, practice, practice!

Are you a mutterer? One way to tell is to think back on how often people ask you to repeat what you've just said. If people ask you fairly often — maybe twice a day or so — there's a good chance you're mumbling. To make sure an interviewer understands you — and to communicate your job-seeker personal brand well — you need to state your words clearly. Not doing so runs the risk of creating a personal brand image that is careless and sloppy — someone who doesn't care about being understood. Or, worse, you could come across as someone who isn't very capable, and that's a definite Job-Seeker Personal Brand Buster™!

One way you can practice is to record yourself reading parts of the front page of the newspaper every day. Then, play it back, and listen to how well you enunciate and pronounce your words. Ask others to listen to your recordings to make sure they can understand everything you say. That will tell you immediately if you're enunciating well enough.

Pace. Do you speak too quickly or too slowly? Either extreme can be a problem. If you speak too fast, the interviewer will have trouble keeping up with your words, and talking fast makes you come across as impatient, nervous, or in a rush. By linking your words together too quickly, the interviewer will probably just stop trying to understand you — a sure sign that communication has broken down. It can be easy to fall into this trap in an interview situation. Let's face it: You're trying to convey as much information about YOU™ as possible in a fairly short period of time, right? But if you try too hard to get everything said, you might just come across as desperate. And that doesn't serve any personal brand.

People also tire quickly if they have to work to keep up with you. Take a cue from U.S. television ads for prescription drugs. After the announcer shares the information the drug company *wants* you to hear — in a patient "explaining" voice — the announcer will suddenly speed up to an unbelievably fast pace when it comes time to share the drug's side effects, speaking-as-if-there-are-no-spacebars-between-his-words. As you can imagine, the advertisers are hoping you'll tune out and/or miss that information entirely even though they have to include it in the commercial because it's required by law.

If you speak too slowly, on the other hand, your interviewer will also most likely get tired, impatient, and bored. Here's a helpful clue: If you find people often finishing your sentences or jumping in to figure out what you're trying to say next, it might be a sign you're a slow talker. Work toward speeding it up just a little, and ask friends to help you determine if your pace is improving.

Volume. In an interview situation, you want to avoid speaking too loudly or too softly. No one likes to be shouted at, so if you speak too loudly, you risk communicating a "bully" or domineering personal Brand Character. This is especially true over the phone. Do you remember a time when you spoke to someone whose vocal volume was so loud that you had to hold the receiver away from your ear? It's uncomfortable and annoying, and that's not the type of person you would want to hire.

On the other hand, speaking too softly is simply pointless. This may sound a bit harsh, but honestly, in an interview situation, you should either speak up … or shut up. Nothing is more tiring than straining to hear what someone is saying, and it doesn't take long before an interviewer will simply give up.

Unfortunately, women are often the guiltiest when it comes to low-volume speaking. I once sat on the board of a not-for-profit organization whose CFO was a very capable woman. However, in board meetings, she spoke so softly while presenting her financial reports that the entire board would literally lean forward to try to hear her. The CEO tried coaching her to speak more loudly, but nothing seemed to work. Out of sheer frustration, she was finally asked to wear a clip microphone on her lapel which she turned on when she wanted to speak. I got the impression she thought this was a bit funny and almost endearing. But it wasn't. All it communicated was a very weak personal brand. In fact, it made some board members even question her ability as a CFO because she just couldn't get past her naturally quiet voice.

If speaking too softly is your challenge, I recommend you pretend that the person you're talking to is far off in a corner of the room (even if the interviewer is only four feet away). In any case, you need to work hard at increasing your volume. Not doing so can be a Personal Brand — and a career — Buster™, and it simply isn't worth it to ignore the problem.

The Power of Emotion. Think about dynamic speakers you've heard. It's the emotions they are able to get across that have everyone on the edge of their seats. Sure, the words they use may have an impact on you, but if those same words were spoken without much color, they would fall flat. A great personal brand builder knows that getting your point across with just the right amount of emotion will get your Audience involved in the message, even if your Audience is simply one interviewer.

Listen to your voice recording again, and ask yourself: What emotions are you broadcasting through your voice patterns? Listen honestly. Is your voice full of energy and enthusiasm, or does it lack commitment? Is your voice convincing when you speak? If you find you have a monotone voice — the kind of voice that sounds humdrum after a while — practice changing the tone, and work at letting the right kinds of emotions come through with your Sound. Again, if this is a particular problem for you, and you have the opportunity to work with a voice coach, it may have a positive impact on your job search. If you're not sure how your emotions carry through your voice, ask others for their opinions.

On the Telephone. All of the aspects of your Sound that we've talked about so far are just as important to your telephone voice as to your in-person voice. Don't underestimate the importance of communicating your job-seeker personal brand through your Sound on the phone. And this applies whether you're phoning an interviewer, an HR representative, a secretary, or a receptionist.

Practicing good phone etiquette with *anyone* is a great Personal Brand Booster™. Courtesy, clarity of tone, and articulating words are key. Here are some great tips to communicate YOU™ on the phone:

- Simple things like always thanking the person on the other end of the line and saying goodbye before hanging up go a long way toward establishing who YOU™ are.

- Practice what you're going to say beforehand, especially if you think you'll need to leave a voicemail message. It helps you to clarify what you really want to say and will prevent you from stumbling over your words.

- Speak clearly but not too quickly. If you leave your name, slow down and spell it out. Then, repeat your telephone number to make sure it's understandable.

Your Sound *Before* the Interview

All of the above suggestions can be used before, during, *and* after an interview, but there are certain strategies for your Sound that you should specifically take care of before your interviews. Don't forget, for example, that your Sound is about more than just your voice, and it can have an impact on your job-seeker personal brand before you even speak to anyone at your target companies.

Your "**Written Sound.**" It's one of the biggest mistakes that job seekers overlook: Forgetting that even though cover letters and resumes are written, they still reflect your Sound, just like they reflect your Look. So, when you prepare your cover letters and resume — which are incredibly important introductions to YOU™ — keep them simple. Leave out large, fancy words. While you may think it makes you sound smart to use big words and share lots of information, those very same things may also make you sound like you're trying too hard.

Read through your cover letters and resume again, and keep the overall "Sound" of your job-seeker personal brand in mind. What is coming through? If it's not the "Sound" you want it to be, what tone would someone with your personal brand use in a letter or resume? Would it be warm? Assertive? Enthusiastic?

Have someone you trust and who knows you well read through your cover letters and resume to let you know if they really reflect YOU™. A friend of mine — who was incredibly fun-loving, gregarious, and charming in person — asked me to read through his application for a job. If I hadn't known him, I would have thought he was a completely different person based on what I read. He sounded incredibly stuffy and pompous! His writing didn't do his personal brand justice at all. So, if you need a hand getting your job-seeker personal brand across in writing, find someone who is a good writer who can help you. Remember: YOU™ will get you the job, but your cover letter and resume are responsible for getting YOU™ the interview.

Your "Virtual Sound." E-mails reflect your written sound just as much as your cover letter and resume. It's a fascinating truth of modern-day communications: We pay close attention to what we write in a letter that will be printed up and signed on a piece of stationery, but we can be very careless when it comes to writing e-mails. Isn't that true? I've seen people agonize over what will be printed on letterhead, but those same folks will send out rapid-fire e-mails without paying much attention to content or errors.

It's critical to remember that your personal brand comes through in your e-mails just as much as it does on the phone, in person, and in your cover letter and resume. And just as with speech, communicating your Sound via e-mail is as much about what you write as it is about how you write it.

For example, do you start your e-mails with a nice greeting, or do you just write a one-line response to the previous question with no sign-off? If you phoned the person you are writing, you wouldn't just state your one-line response and then hang up without a hello or goodbye, would you? It's interesting, but for some reason, we seem to communicate differently in e-mails. But that can be a huge mistake! E-mails run the risk of coming across flippant and rude if we're not careful.

Remember the job-seeker personal brand that you're trying to communicate, and think about how you can use your e-mails to support that. For example, take an extra ten seconds to start and end all e-mails with a simple but nice greeting, as well as a warm closing. It's an opportunity — often before the first interview — to build a professional "connection" with an interviewer. And trust me: You'll certainly stand out from others who take less care with their e-mails. It's just one more way you can build a great job-seeker personal brand in the eyes of your interviewers. This is especially true of e-mails that you send prior to your interview. If your e-mails are off-putting, it will be hard to get past that first impression when it comes time to meet your interviewer in person.

Here are some other things to watch out for in your e-mails:

- You would never dream of sending a cover letter that contains no capital letters or punctuation, but for some reason, a fair number of people do this in e-mails. Professional job-seeker e-mails need to contain capital letters and punctuation, too.

- In your e-mails, include a signature that has your name and telephone number in it. This reminds the interviewer of who you are and makes it easy for the interviewer to contact you. Never require an interviewer to search through your e-mails for the one e-mail in which you included your phone number.

- Be sure to use spell check on all computer communications. With today's technology, spelling errors in interview documents are not acceptable. All that said, don't rely on spell check entirely because it doesn't pick up every mistake. So, be sure to have a careful look yourself before hitting that "send" button.

- If writing isn't your strong suit, admit it, and ask a friend who is a good writer to read through the important e-mails you've written before you send them out.

- Make sure your subject lines are clear and to the point. They should reflect exactly what your e-mail is about. Think of your subject head as a title of a document, which means at a minimum, the first word of your subject line should be capitalized.

- Don't attach any files unless you have been specifically asked to do so. If you don't, your e-mail runs the risk of ending up in an interviewer's spam folder somewhere, and that's definitely not going to get you a job!

- Humor is great to include if you can and if it's consistent with your personal brand, but be careful with jokes. It can sometimes be hard to get the real intention across in an e-mail, so you run the risk of being misunderstood.

- Emoticons might be fun in personal e-mail communications, but don't use them in a professional e-mail, particularly if the e-mail is being sent to an interviewer or if it is at all connected to your job search.

Right *Before* the Interview

Back to your voice, there are two things you can do immediately before your interview to help your Sound considerably:

Wet Your Whistle. This is one of those simple things that can be easy to forget. Didn't bring a bottle of water with you to the interview? That's okay. Accept a glass of water before your interview (if you're offered). It'll keep your vocal cords flexible and strong. This is especially true if you tend to get "dry mouth" when you're nervous. Ask if it's okay to take your glass of water into the interview with you, and sip as necessary. Interviewers don't mind at all, and it's one simple way to make sure your job-seeker personal brand Sound stays strong.

Warm-Up. A chat with the receptionist or others in the waiting room can help to warm up your voice and make you more comfortable. (At the very least, it helps you come across as a friendly person!) Of course, use common sense: Don't start a conversation with someone who's reading or clearly busy with something else. But warming up your voice will avoid the possibility of sounding "croaky" when you finally make it into the interviewer's office.

Your Sound *During* the Interview

If you take the time to work on and improve your Sound before you get into interview situations, you'll be even more ready for a great job interview experience. Still, there are a few more things to watch out for with regard to your Sound when you're actually sitting across from the interviewer's desk. Consider it "showtime," folks!

Talking Too Much. If you tend to talk too much, not letting anybody else get a word in edgewise, it's really important that you learn to stop, breathe, and listen. It's easy to forget to do this when you get excited or nervous, but if you don't, your interviewer will eventually tune you out — and you'll find yourself without a job offer. In fact, people who talk too much can come across as self-centered and unwilling to listen to others, especially if they tend to interrupt. Not a Personal Brand Booster™, that's for sure!

So while you should tell the interviewer as much about you as is reasonable in the interview, you definitely want it to be a *conversation* between two people. How do you do this? Well, for example, besides answering questions about you, don't forget to ask your questions about the company, too. Remember that an interview is a two-way conversation. And don't forget that a few seconds of silence now and then can also be a great Sound.

Not Talking Enough. The opposite is a problem, too. Do you tend to be quiet most of the time? As hard as it may be at first, for the sake of your job-seeker personal brand, it's really important to speak up and participate in conversations — particularly in an interview. You won't get that dream job if you're tight-lipped about yourself or your accomplishments. Learn the balance between bragging about yourself and being overly humble. Ask friends to listen to you talk about your accomplishments and tell you if your confidence is too much or too little. It's all about learning to communicate YOU™ in the best way possible.

Another reminder: The more prepared you are for your interviews, the less likely you are to fall into the trap of being too quiet. Do enough homework so that you're ready to make your points with just the right amount of talking — not too little and not too much.

Stay on Topic. As mentioned earlier, it's important to think of your interview as a conversation between two people. All that said, be careful not to let yourself or the interviewer veer off topic while chatting. It's as much up to you as the interviewer to make sure the most important information about your experience is communicated. If you allow yourself to go off on tangents, you'll lose the valuable time you need to talk about your Unique Strengths, Reasons Why, and Brand Character. Stay focused on the key messages you want to get across, and if you find yourself off in "la-la land," say something like: "Returning to what we were originally talking about…"

Be Polite. Everyday language has gotten more and more relaxed and casual over the past few decades, and that's fine. But remember: *Interview language is different.* Your language in an interview needs to be a bit more formal. For example, answer questions with "yes" rather than "yep" and with "no" rather than "nope." Say "thank you" and "please" when it fits.

What's in a Name? Use the interviewer's name when you first shake hands, saying something like, "Hello, _____, it's great to finally meet you." Simple phrases like that get across a personable "Sound" and establish a relationship from the very start. And it lets the person know that you recognize your interviewer as his or her own personal brand. After all, as they say, everyone's favorite word is their own name, right?

Those Pesky Cell Phones. This is one of those things that you can easily forget about, but your cell phone is also part of your Sound. Be sure to turn off your cell phone before you enter the company's building. Interviewers find it annoying as heck to be interrupted by your phone going off during an interview. On your way to the interview, turn your phone to silent or turn the phone off altogether. If you don't — and you answer the phone — you run the risk of making the interviewer believe you think there's something more pressing or important than getting the job.

And don't even think about talking on your cell phone while you're in the company's waiting room! Remember: The receptionist may be listening to what you have to say to your Aunt Sally and could report it back to the interviewer. If you get a call from another of your target companies, what incriminating information might be overheard? Plus, your cell phone conversation is probably fairly annoying to the receptionist and anyone else sitting in the waiting area.

What Does Your Phone Ring Say about YOU™? Here's a funny cell phone experience I had a while back. I was meeting with a potential executive coaching client who held a very high position in his company. During our meeting — as I sat across from his big mahogany desk inside an office that was as large as a hotel suite with his two personal assistants sitting outside — this executive's cell phone rang. I expected a standard ring tone, befitting of a high-level corporate executive, but that's not what I heard. All of a sudden, I heard this raucously wild hip hop song at full volume! I have to tell you that in a single instant, my impression of this man's personal brand changed drastically. I was shocked because his ring tone wasn't at all what I would have expected for someone of his stature.

As it turns out, his teenage son had played a practical joke on him and changed his ring tone. Once the executive turned off the phone and shared that fact with me, we both had a good laugh. He even admitted that he just didn't have the technical savvy to figure out how to change the ring tone back, so all he could do was continuously apologize for it.

While it was a really funny experience that still makes me chuckle when I think about it, I realized that even the ring tones people choose on their cell phones can have an impact on their personal brands.

Your Sound *After* the Interview

The same Sound tips we've talked about throughout this chapter still apply just as much after an interview and in a follow-up interview as they do before and during an interview. Don't let your "Sound" go just because you've gotten to that coveted second interview or because you've developed a more comfortable relationship with the interviewer. Stay the course, and keep up the consistency with your job-seeker personal brand Sound. It's key to represent your personal brand well in *all* of your communications from e-mails to telephone calls to in-person meetings.

> **Your Thank You Note.** As mentioned in the Actions chapter, you absolutely, positively should write a thank you note to the interviewer within 24 hours after your interview. Statistics show that only about 10% of applicants write a thank you after an interview, so it's clearly a great way to stand out. And, the more you can distinguish yourself in your follow-up thank you note, the more memorable your job-seeker personal brand will be with the interviewer. All of that means you'll have a better chance of getting hired! In fact, if you're in the "maybe" pile when you leave the interview, a well thought-out thank you could easily move you to the "yes" pile.
>
> Here are some tips for making your follow-up thank you a powerful statement for YOU™:
>
> - Personalize your thank you note. If you send a "cookie-cutter" thank you that sounds like it's the same one you send to everyone after an interview, you could just as easily move from the "maybe" pile to the "rejected" pile. So, no cutting and pasting! Mention something specific that happened in the interview to help the interviewer remember you.

- Express your interest in the job, and be enthusiastic about it! Be willing to show your excitement and passion.

- Mention why you believe you're a great fit for the position, maybe even repeating a key Unique Strength or Reason Why that you talked about during the interview.

- If you interviewed with more than one person, send each of them a separate thank you.

- Triple-check the thank you note to make sure everything is correct — especially the interviewer's name and title.

- If you know the company is going to make a quick hiring decision, send your thank you via e-mail. If they're going to take a couple of weeks or longer to hire someone, stand out even more by sending your thank you note by snail mail. These days, snail mail is unexpected, so it can help you be remembered.

The Subsequent E-mail Trap. Don't suddenly get casual with your e-mails to the interviewer or anyone else at the company. As one of the recruiters I interviewed cautions: "Don't start forwarding jokes or funny e-mails to the interviewer or disclosing information about your personal life even if you begin to feel more comfortable with that person. It's critical to keep a professional relationship with the interviewer no matter how friendly you may have become." Acting too familiar too quickly could undermine all that you've worked hard to accomplish. Yes, you do want the interviewer to like you, but you don't want to lose the job to someone else when you're that close just because you've accidentally crossed the line.

Your "Sound" Marketing Plan

So, how does your job-seeker personal brand sound now? It's time to explore the Sound portion of your Job-Seeker Personal Brand Marketing Plan. Let's tune in to our two colleagues to see how each of them will use Sound to communicate their personal brands during their job search process.

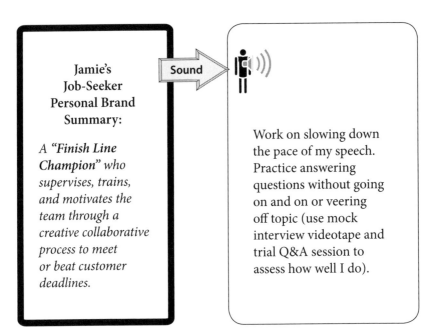

Jamie's
Job-Seeker
Personal Brand
Summary:

A *"Finish Line Champion"* who supervises, trains, and motivates the team through a creative collaborative process to meet or beat customer deadlines.

Sound

Work on slowing down the pace of my speech. Practice answering questions without going on and on or veering off topic (use mock interview videotape and trial Q&A session to assess how well I do).

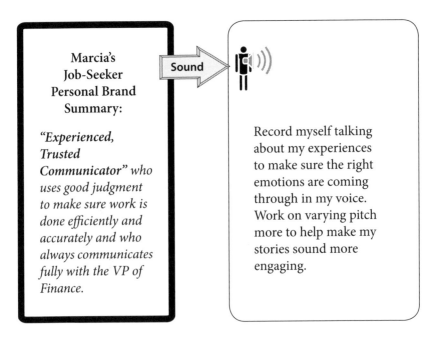

Marcia's
Job-Seeker
Personal Brand
Summary:

"Experienced, Trusted Communicator" who uses good judgment to make sure work is done efficiently and accurately and who always communicates fully with the VP of Finance.

Sound

Record myself talking about my experiences to make sure the right emotions are coming through in my voice. Work on varying pitch more to help make my stories sound more engaging.

Okay, you know the drill—it's your turn. What is your Sound Marketing Plan? What steps will you take to make sure your Sound reflects the best brand YOU™?

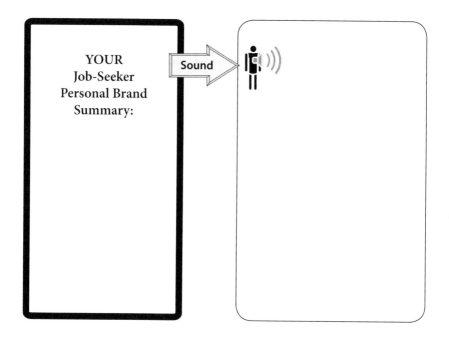

YOUR
Job-Seeker
Personal Brand
Summary:

Sound

“ *Many sounds
— not just music —
absolutely have the power
to influence us.* ”

Communicate it

16

Thoughts

Job-Seeker Personal Brand Marketing Plan Activity #5

Whether you think you can or whether you think you can't, you're right.

— Henry Ford, Founder of the Ford Motor Company

I really believe I've saved the best for last when it comes to the five activities that communicate your job-seeker personal brand: your Thoughts. Of the five activities that most successfully get across your personal brand, this is the one that can impact every other activity in your Job-Seeker Personal Brand Marketing Plan. Your Thoughts can influence your Actions, your Reactions, your Look, and your Sound, so they can have a profound impact on the success of your job search.

Unfortunately, looking for a job is high on the list of situations that can cause stress. It's right up there not far behind the death of a spouse, an illness, and moving. The lack of certainty that comes with a job search can be unsettling and challenging. Yet, every year, millions of people around the world find themselves changing jobs. So, the trick is learning to successfully manage this stress, and one of the best ways to deal with it is to take control of your Thoughts.

Time and time again, I've witnessed job seekers struggle to find a job because they have negative Thoughts about the job search process, while those who take on a positive mindset find a great job much more quickly. So, let's explore how changing your Thoughts can take the edge off of job-hunting stress.

The Truth About Thoughts

What I'm about to write may sound a bit crazy to you, but bear with me a minute. In the 1600s, Galileo — who is today considered the "Father of Modern Science" — was interrogated for 18 days straight, tortured, imprisoned, and called a heretic. He was then placed under house arrest by the Inquisition for the rest of his life until he died, blind, at the age of 78. He was even buried without a proper monument. What horrible crime had Galileo committed that brought on this brutal treatment?

> He wrote and gave lectures supporting the belief that
> the earth revolves around the sun.

Can you imagine that? Today, we know it's a fact that the earth revolves around the sun — we couldn't imagine it any other way — but in Galileo's time, that idea was considered outrageous.

I tell you Galileo's story in the hope that you'll open your mind as you read this chapter and consider these next words as possible, even if they challenge everything you've believed up to this point. Many scientists firmly believe that in the future, the following three words will be as common and as accepted an idea as our sun-centered solar system is today. Here they are:

Thoughts are Things

It's true: Science is beginning to prove that Thoughts exist in this world in a very real way — that Thoughts are made up of energy, just like a flower, an animal, or the human body. Even though our Thoughts may not be "seen" like a shoe or "touched" like a feather, Thoughts absolutely, positively exist. (Think about it: You can't see air either, but it's definitely there, right?) We can prove that the physical brain exists, but the "thinker" — the part of us that actually thinks our Thoughts — is still pretty much a mystery to us.

So, let's focus in this chapter on the power that your Thoughts can have on the consistent communication of your personal brand during your job search and beyond. Just like you can make choices as to which pen you use or what you do with your computer, you have choices as to how you use your Thoughts to get the job you want.

Of course, the "things" in our lives that we normally see and touch are usually created by someone else — Toshiba made my computer, for example, and Mont Blanc made my pen. But to me, the most exciting thing about our Thoughts is this: *We* create them. Your thoughts are 100% yours — no one else can create them for you. And that's great news because it means you have ultimate control over your Thoughts. You and you alone are responsible for both the Thoughts you think as well as the outcome of those Thoughts — from start to finish.

In fact, if you think about it (every pun intended!), you actually have more control over your Thoughts than you do over a lot of what makes up your Look and your Sound. Even though your brain may have some involvement in your thinking, your body isn't really involved with *what* you think. So, you can change your Thoughts at will. It may not be obvious how to do this at first, but your Thoughts offer you an enormous opportunity to impact each and every aspect of your Job-Seeker Personal Brand Marketing Plan.

In short, you can take full control of your personal brand — and your job search — through your Thoughts. It's just a matter of knowing how and making the effort.

Thoughts Are Like Chain Smoking

Psychologists believe each of us thinks about 60,000 Thoughts every day. That's 3,750 Thoughts per waking hour — a lot by anyone's estimation! But have you ever taken the time to do an "inventory" of your Thoughts? Stop and consider that for a moment. What kinds of Thoughts are you creating every hour?

Psychologists also estimate that 95% to 98% of those 60,000 thoughts each day are repeated the next day, and the next day, and the next day. That means only 2% to 5% of our Thoughts are ever really different from one day to the next. Our Thoughts are like habits. We stick with the same Thought patterns and stay in the same kind of "Thought rut" day in and day out. You'd think we'd get tired of the same Thoughts, wouldn't you? But obviously, we don't even notice we're thinking the same things over and over. We don't really stop to consider what our heads are filled with day after day.

If you're like most people, your mind has probably picked up some bad habits over the years. It's no wonder that we get into patterns in our lives that we can't seem to shake. In fact, did you ever stop to chew on the idea that it might be your Thoughts that are responsible for negative patterns that play out over and over in your life?

Actually, it's nothing but a good old fashioned cause-and-effect relationship at work here. Your Thoughts are the cause, and your job, your career, your life, your relationships — and your personal brand — are the effect. If you want to change the "effect" — the outcome — then you need to change the "cause" — your Thoughts. Simple, isn't it?

Okay, okay, I know it *sounds* simple, but I'm sure you're asking: "How do I actually DO that — especially when it comes to something as stressful and potentially challenging as a job search?" Well, just like a chain smoker or someone who drinks too much, it's up to you to change your thinking habits. It takes concentration, but remember that you — and only you — have the power to control what you think about at any point in time. If you don't take charge of what you think, you'll just continue the same old habits that could have a negative impact on your job search.

There are three key steps to taking charge of your Thoughts and getting better job search results:

1. Become aware of your Thoughts.

2. Turn negative Thoughts into positive Thoughts.

3. Embrace positive thinking as a new habit.

Become Aware of Your Thoughts

To change your Thoughts, the first step is to begin paying attention to what you're thinking day in and day out. Of those 3,750 Thoughts screaming in your head every hour, how many of them are you actually conscious of? What's rattling around in your brain all day?

Here's an exercise to help you become more aware of what you're thinking about:

1. Gather two highlighters of different colors, a few pieces of lined paper, and a writing pen.

2. Set a timer for five minutes. Then, put your pen to paper, and start writing everything that comes to your mind. Write down every single Thought that pops into your head for those five minutes, and try not to let your pen stop. Don't worry about

what you've written or whether it makes sense — no one has to ever read it but you.

3. Once the five minutes is up, read the Thoughts you've written. Take the two colored highlighters, and highlight every Thought related to "work" in one color and every Thought related to "personal" in a different color.

4. Then, go back and re-read all of your Thoughts once again. This time, with your pen, underline all of the negative Thoughts and circle all of the positive Thoughts.

5. Now, sit back and look at the outcome. First, which color do you see the most on your pages — the color you chose for work Thoughts, or the color you chose for personal Thoughts? What types of Thoughts most prevail in your mind? Likewise, are there more underlines (negative Thoughts) or more circles (positive Thoughts) on your pages? Are your negative Thoughts more related to work/your job search or to your personal life? What do you think about positively?

From that exercise, what did you learn about your Thoughts? It's a great way to become more aware of the content of the 60,000 Thoughts you have in a day, and that kind of awareness is the first key step toward changing your Thoughts. If you've discovered that you have a lot of negative Thoughts, don't let your worry about it create yet another negative Thought! Just keep reading, and you'll learn many great tips about how to stop your thinking from getting you down.

Turn Negative Thoughts into Positive Thoughts

Once you're aware of the content of your Thoughts, the second step to managing your Thoughts is conditioning yourself to turn negative Thoughts into positive Thoughts. Maybe that sounds hard to do, but there are people all across the globe who manage to keep their Thoughts positive rather than negative.

Do you know people who are just naturally happy — people whose lives seem to always come together for them and fall into place? They have the perfect family, the perfect job, the perfect life. You know the kind of people I'm talking about, right? Well, I believe there's one thing that unites them all: They regularly think positive Thoughts. These people see the glass as half-full instead of half-empty. Guaranteed.

The positive results you see in their lives and in their personal brands are internally driven. People like that just naturally think about how things will turn out *well*, and their Thoughts become a reality. They don't focus on drama, details, or problems. They focus on what the positive outcome will be, and you can see the result of their Thoughts in their lives every single day. What they think actually becomes real.

So, how are your Thoughts impacting *your* life, *your* career … and *your* job search? Are you one of those people who wake up in the morning and say, "Ugh! Another day. I've got yet another job interview this afternoon, but I don't know why I even try. I already know I won't get the job." And, of course, because that Thought plays over and over in your mind for the next 24 hours, it's a self-fulfilling prophecy. You proved yourself right, but what did you gain from that?

Instead, what if you changed that initial Thought into something positive? What if the first thing you said to yourself when you woke up was, "Whoo hoo — another day! The job interview I have this afternoon is going to be great. I look forward to letting the interviewer know what I have to offer the company and finding out what the company has to offer me. I know how I want my personal brand to be perceived, so I'm primed and ready. It's going to be a great day!" Think about it: If you could start the day with that Thought, how different would your day be?

And here's the cool thing: Even if you make a positive statement before you fully believe it, you will eventually begin to believe it. If you just allow for that small opening of possibility that you *could* have that dream job, the door will soon swing wide open for you if you consistently think positively about it.

I'm not advocating that you walk around with the attitude of an over-the-top game show host, but expecting the worst will definitely deliver just that: the worst.

Homework Assignment

Every morning this week when you wake up, condition yourself to let the first thing that pops into your head be a positive thought. I guarantee you that, after doing this regularly for a while, you'll be amazed what a difference it makes in the outlook — and even outcome — of your day!

Does thinking more positively sound challenging to you? The truth is that managing your Thoughts is far from rocket science or magic. It's actually incredibly simple, and — as we said earlier — you are in charge. For example:

- Do you want your interviewers to perceive, think, and feel that your personal brand is "creative?" Then, think creative Thoughts about interviews and your personal brand.

- Do you want your interviewers to treat you nicely? Then, think nice thoughts about your interviewers.

- Do you want to feel more at peace during the job search process? Then, think more peaceful thoughts.

Try This Exercise

Let's do something similar to the writing exercise you did earlier, but this time, let's focus on two questions that are directly related to interviewing. Grab a pen and some paper, and find a quiet place to sit down. Take a deep breath, and ask yourself these questions:

- What are my Thoughts about interviewing?
- How do I feel about interviewing?

As you focus on these two questions, write down everything that comes to mind, and don't stop until you've written for about three minutes.

Now, go back and look at what you wrote. How many of your Thoughts around interviewing are negative? How many of your feelings about interviews are fearful and based on worry? By contrast, how many of your Thoughts and feelings are positive? If you're like most people, the idea of an interview produces more negative Thoughts than positive and can plant a lot of fear into your heart. How do you change that?

Remember: Thoughts are things. They exist in the world in a real way. If you find yourself thinking, "I'll never get a great job," guess what? You won't. Instead, take all of that negative energy and use it to think Thoughts like, "The best job for me is only an interview away." Replace each negative thought with a positive one. As the famous baseball player Babe Ruth once said, "Never let the fear of striking out get in your way." You must envision and *know* that a positive outcome will be the ultimate result of your job search. That means accepting temporary setbacks as just that — temporary. They are simply there to help you learn, grow, and move closer to your goal.

Embrace Positive Thinking as a New Habit

Let's move on to our third step toward taking charge of your Thoughts — embracing positive thinking as a new habit. I can almost hear you saying, "Brenda, I've heard that stuff about controlling your Thoughts before, but it's just too hard!" A Buddhist monk in Thailand once told me that our minds can be like an untamed monkey, always jumping about actively, running here and there. To train it, you have to learn to reel in the monkey, as though it were on a chain, until it's fully within your control. You can choose when to reel in your "monkey mind" and when to let it run wild again. It's your mind, after all! Let's put it this way: Either you control your mind and your Thoughts, or your mind and your Thoughts control you. I know which one I prefer. How about you?

Grabbing Your Monkey Mind By the Tail

There are a lot of ways you can take control of your Thoughts and reel in that monkey mind. Grab it by the tail, and make it your pet — not the other way around. Then and only then can positive thinking become your way of being — like those people you know who seem to have "charmed" lives. I'm not saying that nothing painful will ever happen to you again, but your attitude about what happens to you will become positive enough that you will get through difficult situations easier and change your circumstances sooner rather than later.

1. **Take Charge!** Tell your mind that you're the one in control here and that you simply won't allow any negative Thoughts to interfere with building the personal brand you want and getting you the job you deserve.

2. **Switch from Negative to Positive.** If you find that your Thoughts are running amuck with fear, wondering, questioning, and "what if" scenarios when it comes to finding a new job, start training yourself to switch your thinking to something positive. Make a list of the happiest moments in your life, but write them in detail. For example, don't just write: "The day I got the salesperson of the month award for my division." Instead, create a list that will really help you when you're feeling down by reminding you of

exactly how you felt during that proud moment. Write something like: "The day I got the salesperson of the month award from my division, my supervisor called me into the conference room and congratulated me in front of the whole team. Everyone applauded, and it was a day I felt like I was walking on air. I was so proud and felt like I'd accomplished a lot. It was clear that my boss and my team really appreciated the work I'd done."

Then, when you need to switch your thinking from something negative, focus your mind on one of the positive memories on your list. Relive it as best you can. Close your eyes for a moment, and remember any sights, sounds, smells, textures, or tastes to help you go back to that happier time. The more you practice this exercise, the more quickly you will be able to transform your negative Thoughts into positive ones. In fact, eventually, all you will have to do is think "my salesperson of the month award," for example, and you'll automatically shift your focus and get rid of those negative Thoughts.

3. **Set Goals for Changing Your Thought Patterns**. Your goals should be achievable but realistic, and you should be able to measure them in some way. This way, you'll know exactly when you've reached each of them. For example: "Between now and 3:00 p.m., every time I catch myself thinking a non-personal-brand-building Thought, I'm going to switch my thinking to _____ instead." It takes focus and effort, but can you see how this can train your monkey mind over time?

4. **Reward Yourself for Reaching Your Goals and Thinking Positive Brand-Building Thoughts**. Take an inventory at the end of each day. If the majority of your Thoughts were positive ones, treat yourself to a visit to Starbucks on the way home, or take yourself to a movie. Once your mind catches on that you're going to be rewarded for thinking positive Thoughts, it will be much easier to tame. Eventually, thinking positively will simply become a way of life for you, and remaining positive before, during, and after job interviews will simply be your natural way of being.

5. **Affirm What You Want**. You have probably heard about positive affirmations, and maybe you've even used them in the past. They really are a powerful way to alter your Thoughts. Think of all of the positive affirmations you can say about yourself in the job search process. For example:

"I do a great job of communicating my personal brand in interviews."

"I come across as very charismatic in interviews, and interviewers see me as confident and professional."

"I am hired by a great company for a job I enjoy that will help me grow both personally and professionally."

It's important that every affirmation be written or spoken in the present, as if it is already truth. That's the point! You don't have to fully believe the affirmation for it to begin to do its good work — impacting the way you think — but the key is to strive to believe these affirmations more and more as you read and/or write them.

Make affirmations a regular part of your day. Read your affirmations first thing in the morning, at lunch time, and right before you go to sleep. If you can, read them out loud, and really "feel" what it's like to have that affirmation become real. Envision yourself as your life will be when these statements are reality. Some people even write each affirmation in a notebook 20 or more times per day. Do what it takes to get your mind wrapped around the image of you living the life you want and having the job you desire.

Your Thoughts *Before* the Interview

If you want to have more control of your Thoughts *during* an interview, it's important to work on your Thoughts *before* the interview. The more positive you keep your Thoughts about an interview beforehand, the more confident and relaxed you'll be when you're in an interviewer's office.

Positive Self-Talk. When you feel anxious, angry, or worried, you can bet it's a result of negative Thoughts. Psychologists say that one of the best ways to move yourself into a better state of mind is to talk yourself out of it. Just hearing your own inner voice telling you to stay calm can help take the edge off of the situation. It's a way of soothing your monkey mind and affirming the positive, and you can even do it right before you walk into the interviewer's office. But it's even better to use this skill to talk to yourself positively about the interview in the days before the appointment, the same day as the interview, and again while you sit in the waiting room. You'll be amazed by how much this can help to keep your nerves — and negative Thoughts — in check.

Face Your Fears. What are you worried about that might happen in an interview, and how can you turn those worries into a positive? For example, if your Thoughts are telling you that a potential employer might think you're overqualified for a job, replace that Thought with the belief that they'll hire you anyway with the intention of promoting you faster than usual. Maybe your worry Thought is that they'll think you have too little experience? Prepare to share with the interviewer how you can bring a fresh perspective from the younger generation into the company and help them to understand a younger customer base. Being prepared will help to calm your fearful Thoughts considerably.

Keep Your Personal Brand Summary Near. Stash your job-seeker personal brand summary in your wallet or purse or maybe even post it on your computer or refrigerator. When you do that, it will stay top of mind at all times. This will help you to keep your Thoughts where they belong — on your job goal. Choose two or three key words from your summary, and repeat them to yourself whenever your confidence or positive Thoughts begin to fade. You can even do this in a split second before (and during) the interview to bring your Thoughts and energy back to where you want them to be.

The "Picture" of Success

Top actors and athletes often say that they envision their success. They actually picture themselves getting the role, giving a great performance, winning the game, or crossing the finish line first. Many of them swear by this method for not only staying positively focused before a big event, but for turning what they picture into reality.

Let's apply this to you finding and getting the job you want. Try playing out "tomorrows" in your mind. What does a successful interview look like? Play it out in your head as if you're watching a movie. Really "feel" the emotions of doing a great job in an interview. How are interviewers responding to YOU™? How are YOU™ responding to them? How are you presenting yourself before, during, and after your interviews? How do you look when you walk into the interviewer's office? How does it feel when the interviewer recognizes what YOU™ have to offer? What does it feel like to be charismatic? What does it feel like to actually enjoy an interview and walk out feeling terrific?

Visualizing yourself successful in interviews will help you become excited about them. Don't overlook this as a great tool! The more energy and enthusiasm you bring to the table, the more the interviewer will feel that energy. If you walk into the room feeling defeated or depressed from the start — even if you try to hide it — I guarantee you the interviewer will feel that, too. But with sincere passion and an upbeat attitude, you have a strong chance of getting the job, even if someone else in the running has better qualifications.

Picture yourself successfully putting your Job-Seeker Personal Brand Marketing Plan into effect and being offered the best possible job with the salary and perks you desire. You can fast-forward and visualize yourself in the job you want, too. What does it feel like to be really excited about the work you do? The key is to turn your Thoughts into activities, and make your vision real. It *is* in your control, and the more you are truly able to sense this as reality in your mind, the closer you will be to making it reality in your life and in your career.

Your Thoughts *During* the Interview

During the interview itself, you will want to keep your mind on the conversation. So, it's key to prepare as much as possible before the interview in order to maintain a positive attitude *during* the interview. In other words, don't wait until you are sitting with the interviewer to try to have positive Thoughts. Remember: Practice makes perfect, so if you want to have positive Thoughts during the interview, you need to practice beforehand.

Focus on Your Audience. Even if you have been working on taming your monkey mind, old habits die hard, and you may find negative Thoughts creeping in on you while you're in an interview. If this happens, quickly bring yourself back to the moment, focusing on the interviewer and how you can fill the company's Needs. Remember: Your personal brand won't work unless it fills the Needs of your Audience! So, the more you focus on your Audience, the less you will focus on negative Thoughts, like the mistake you might have made 30 seconds ago.

Reactive Thoughts. Keep in mind that Thoughts are also Reactions, just like physical Reactions. Are your Thought Reactions out of control? When something unexpected happens in an interview, you may try to control what you say and do, but do your Thoughts go wild? Do you immediately jump to conclusions or become frustrated with yourself or the interviewer inside your head?

This kind of Thought Reaction is natural, and I'm definitely not suggesting you should never get angry or that you should try to suppress your emotions. But think seriously about how these Thought Reactions are serving you, especially if you end up "shouting" at yourself or someone else in your mind for days on end as a result. It's easy to get eaten up by emotions in your mind, but that robs you of a lot of energy and only serves to keep you focused on negative Thoughts.

The next time you have a knee-jerk Thought Reaction, catch yourself. Work on letting go of the negative emotion about the situation as quickly as possible. Otherwise, you will let the situation control you, rather than the other way around. Stop thinking in terms of who's right and who's wrong. If you're wasting your time on negative Thoughts just because you believe you'll win an argument, you've already lost. If an interviewer doesn't think you're right for a job or doesn't choose you due to a mistaken impression of you, let it go and move on to a company that can truly appreciate you. Remember that just as you have the power to control your physical Reactions, you can also control your Thought Reactions.

Your Thoughts *After* the Interview

If you let them, your Thought Reactions can "eat at you" long after the interview. Do you obsess about what went wrong when you don't hear from a company right away? Do you get depressed when you don't get a particular job? It's natural to feel disappointment when you don't get a job you hoped for, but be careful with the direction of your Thoughts. They can run amuck and go into those negative spaces again, telling you that you're not qualified enough or that you'll never get the kind of job you want. Don't allow that!

Continue to bring yourself back to positive Thoughts. Practice Thoughts of acceptance: "The best job is out there for me, and everything is lining up just right for it to come to me at just the right time." Also, find humor in the situation, and don't take yourself too seriously. It will help you to keep your Thoughts in check and keep your eyes on the goal.

However You Slice It: Negative Thoughts are Negative Things

Still not convinced that Thoughts are things? Whether or not you can completely buy into the science of Thought, no matter how you look at it, life is frankly just a lot more satisfying when you stay positive and in control of what you think. And it's hard to argue with the fact that people with negative attitudes are simply a lot less enjoyable to have as friends, employees, or business partners. There isn't any benefit in communicating a negative personal brand, and negativity will do nothing to help you get any kind of job. No matter how much work you put into the other aspects of your brand, negative Thoughts will prevent you from fully making YOU™ a reality. Employers will never perceive, think, and feel good about your personal brand as long as negative Thoughts are in the way.

As the world becomes more aware of the power of our Thoughts, more books and films like *The Law of Attraction* and *The Secret* will enter the mainstream. Today, it's becoming more accepted to believe that our lives are really just reflections of our attitudes and Thoughts. We're beginning to see that simple changes within our minds can create real change in our lives and, collectively, in the world.

Your "Thoughts" Marketing Plan

So, how will you work on your Thoughts in your Job-Seeker Personal Brand Marketing Plan? Let's check in with our two colleagues to see what they're going to do to take charge of their Thoughts. Then, it will be your turn to complete your Thoughts Marketing Plan.

Jamie's
Job-Seeker
Personal Brand
Summary:

A *"Finish Line Champion"* who supervises, trains, and motivates the team through a creative collaborative process to meet or beat customer deadlines.

Reward myself weekly by going to a movie if I think positively about my job search and my career future at least 80% of the time.

Marcia's
Job-Seeker
Personal Brand
Summary:

"Experienced, Trusted Communicator" who uses good judgment to make sure work is done efficiently and accurately and who always communicates fully with the VP of Finance.

Practice making my first morning thought a positive one. Work with daily positive affirmations, specifically: "I am appreciated at work and fulfilled in my career."

Okay, it's your turn to complete the last portion of your Marketing Plan. How will you turn your Thoughts from negative to positive and energize your job search?

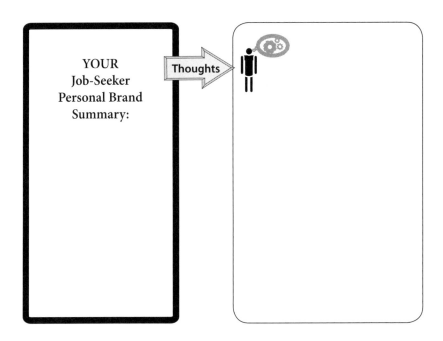

You did it — you've completed all five activities of your Job-Seeker Personal Brand Marketing Plan. You're now ready to pull together your entire Marketing Plan. This is the heart and soul of communicating your personal brand.

You must envision and know that a positive outcome will be the ultimate result of your job search.

"They're complaining about the scarcity of
decent jobs!"

Communicate it

Job-Seeker
Personal Brand Marketing Plan

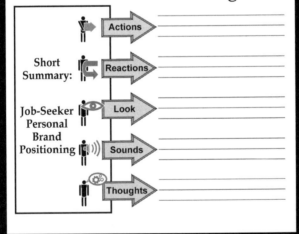

Step 2

17

Your Complete Job-Seeker Personal Brand Marketing Plan

Good plans shape good decisions. That's why good planning helps make elusive dreams come true.

— Lester Robert Bittel, Author

You've carefully defined your personal brand using the six elements that make up YOU™. You've looked in-depth at all five activities that make up your Job-Seeker Personal Brand Marketing Plan. Now, it's time to combine all of the activities together to finalize your full job-search Marketing Plan. Pulling together how you will communicate your personal brand before, during, and after interviews through your Actions, Reactions, Look, Sound, and Thoughts is key to successfully mastering the job search process. This is where true success comes in the form of the job offer you want.

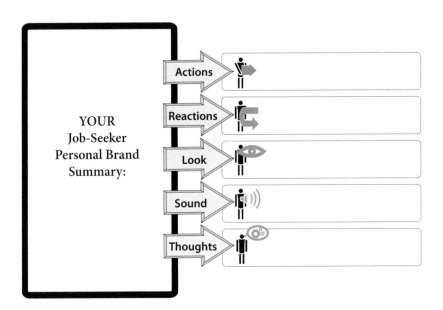

Take a look at the completed Marketing Plans for Jamie and Marcia on the pages that follow. This is how they plan to work on their Actions, Reactions, Look, Sound, and Thoughts to drive a positive outcome in their job search.

As you look at our colleagues' Marketing Plans, what comes to mind? Do you see a full picture of how both of these job seekers are taking charge of their individual job searches?

As you look at their plans, what do they tell you about your own job-seeker Marketing Plan? Do you want to make any adjustments to your Plan as you review their examples? Once you see all of your five Marketing Plan activities together, does anything else come to mind that you can add to your Plan that would strengthen each activity? Will each of your plans move you closer to YOU™ getting that dream job?

Jamie's Job-Seeker Personal Brand Marketing Plan

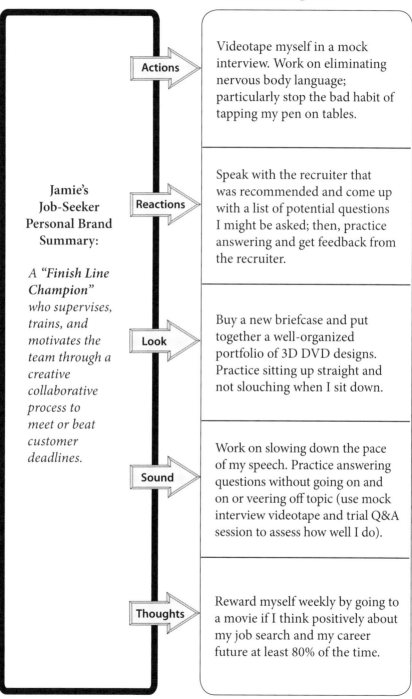

Actions

Videotape myself in a mock interview. Work on eliminating nervous body language; particularly stop the bad habit of tapping my pen on tables.

Jamie's Job-Seeker Personal Brand Summary:

A "Finish Line Champion" who supervises, trains, and motivates the team through a creative collaborative process to meet or beat customer deadlines.

Reactions

Speak with the recruiter that was recommended and come up with a list of potential questions I might be asked; then, practice answering and get feedback from the recruiter.

Look

Buy a new briefcase and put together a well-organized portfolio of 3D DVD designs. Practice sitting up straight and not slouching when I sit down.

Sound

Work on slowing down the pace of my speech. Practice answering questions without going on and on or veering off topic (use mock interview videotape and trial Q&A session to assess how well I do).

Thoughts

Reward myself weekly by going to a movie if I think positively about my job search and my career future at least 80% of the time.

Marcia's Job-Seeker Personal Brand Marketing Plan

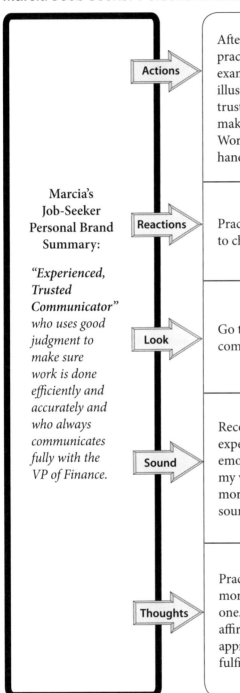

Marcia's Job-Seeker Personal Brand Summary:

"Experienced, Trusted Communicator" who uses good judgment to make sure work is done efficiently and accurately and who always communicates fully with the VP of Finance.

Actions

After first interview experience, practice storytelling and sharing examples from the past that illustrate self-management, trustworthiness, and ability to make strong decisions.
Work on strengthening handshake.

Reactions

Practice "poker face" in response to challenging questions.

Look

Go to department store for complimentary makeup lesson.

Sound

Record myself talking about my experiences to make sure the right emotions are coming through in my voice. Work on varying pitch more to help make my stories sound more engaging.

Thoughts

Practice making my first morning thought a positive one. Work with daily positive affirmations, specifically: "I am appreciated at work and fulfilled in my career."

YOUR Job-Seeker Personal Brand Marketing Plan

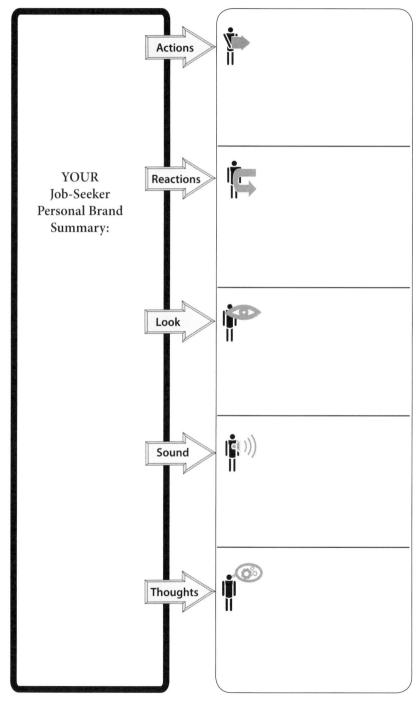

Putting Your Marketing Plan Into Action

As we've said, putting your Job-Seeker Personal Brand Marketing Plan into action is about building a connection with your interviewers. But it can even go beyond that. Every single time you come in contact with anyone who works at one of your target companies, you're building a relationship with that company. Every meeting, phone call, e-mail, or letter is a chance to communicate the powerhouse personal brand you've worked so hard to define and develop. You never know what might come of a "chance" meeting here or there when you could be introduced to someone who knows an employee or executive at one of your target companies. So, make every moment count, and be consistent in communicating your job-seeker personal brand day in and day out with your Actions, Reactions, Look, Sound, and Thoughts.

That's what both Jamie and Marcia did, and it paid off. They were each able to establish a connection with their target companies that got them the jobs they wanted. They did their research and learned about the companies so that they could define a job-seeker personal brand that met their Audience's Needs. Then, they worked on communicating their personal brands to make a great impression in their interviews. Today, they're both doing very well in their new positions where their contributions are valued.

What about you? You've defined your personal brand and put together a plan to communicate it regularly to help you get the job you really want. You're now armed with what you need to succeed in building a powerful personal brand and creating that all-important connection with an interviewer. There's just one more step left to help turn your job-seeker personal brand into the key that unlocks the door to a fulfilling job and a great future. Let's do some troubleshooting and make sure you don't *damage* this personal brand called YOU™ as you continue your job hunt.

You're now armed with what you need to succeed in building a powerful personal brand and creating that all-important connection with an interviewer.

Step 3
Avoid Damaging it

Job-Seeker
Personal
Brand Busters™

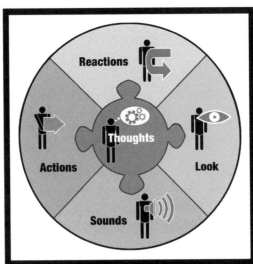

18

Job-Seeker Personal Brand Busters™

Learn from the mistakes of others — you can never live long enough to make them all yourself.

> — John Luther Long, Author of the short story "Madame Butterfly"

You may never have heard of Job-Seeker Personal Brand Busters™ before, but they are the critical last step in assuring your personal brand lands you the exact position you want in your desired company. Learning how to avoid these Busters™ can make the difference between "we'll be in touch" and "welcome to the company!"

So, what do I mean by "Job-Seeker Personal Brand Busters™?" Simply put, they're the same five activities we talked about in Step 2 — your Actions, Reactions, Look, Sound, and Thoughts. But this time, it's the flipside of what we discussed in the chapters you just finished. These Busters™ are what you *don't* want to do during your job search when it comes to your Actions, Reactions, Look, Sound, and Thoughts.

If you're not aware of them, Job-Seeker Personal Brand Busters™ can damage all the work you've done so far to build the personal brand you desire. As Benjamin Franklin once said, "It takes many good deeds to build a good reputation and only one bad one to lose it." These Busters can lead you to bomb in your interviews, lose out on jobs you're applying for, or perhaps never even get interviews in the first place!

My Job-Seeker Personal Brand Busters™ Collection

There are more Job-Seeker Personal Brand Busters™ than we could possibly count.* In fact, through my 25+ years of hiring new employees at major multinational corporations all across the globe, my work as a professional career coach, and hours of discussions and interviews with dozens of human resources experts and recruiters from numerous industries, I have collected and developed an extensive list of Job-Seeker Personal Brand Busters™.

I took this full list of Personal Brand Busters™ to human resources professionals, hiring managers, and recruiting experts from companies around the world. These folks have seen it all! They know the most common—and most damaging—mistakes we all make during the process of looking for a job. That's why I asked them to tell me which of these culprits they think are the "baddest of the bad." Many outstanding professionals took the time and energy to contribute to the list I'm about to share with you.

If you can bypass these worst Busters, you're well on your way to a fulfilling new job. We have divided them into categories based on our five Job-Seeker Personal Brand Marketing Plan activities—four each for Actions, Reactions, Look, Sound, and Thoughts.

What these Busters are all about is helping you to learn from the mistakes of other interviewees who have gone before you. The more you know what to do before, during, and after an interview—as well as what *not* to do—the better off YOU™ will be in your job search. And that will help you leapfrog from where you are now to the ultimate goal of hearing the words: "You're hired!"

Job-Seeker Personal Brand Busters™ are common job-seeker pitfalls or traps you might be falling into right now without even knowing it. Once you're aware of them, you have to keep a watchful eye out for them because they can be like stealth bombers—often under your conscious radar. And once you've learned to master them, it's like walking through a mine field without worry! You'll have the confidence to know you're not committing the worst job-seeker sins, and you'll feel great about your interviews.

Let's be honest: Every one of us looking for a job is guilty of a few Job-Seeker Personal Brand Busters™ from time to time. But knowledge is power. The more you know about these Busters, the more you will know how to avoid them, and the more you will become aware of any of your own Busters as you put your Marketing Plan into action.

Keep in mind that this list is not the "final" list of Job-Seeker Personal Brand Busters™ by any means. In fact, there really is no end to the potential list of Job-Seeker Personal Brand Busters™ that might rear their ugly heads as you go through the job search process. You will definitely come up with other Busters that are unique to your situation. If you do, write them down, and start your own list.

How do you know when you've come across a Job-Seeker Personal Brand Buster™?

1. Recognize when you've made a blunder before, during, or after an interview, and make note of it. That's the best way to avoid making the same mistake over again … and it's the beginning of your own Job-Seeker Personal Brand Busters™ list.

2. Watch other job seekers and talk with them to find out what they have done or said that might have hurt their job search. You'll learn a lot about how to avoid damaging your own job-seeker personal brand.

The Job-Seeker Personal Brand Busters™ laid out in the next chapter will work for anyone in the job search process who wants to come across as professional, confident, reliable, and in control before, during, and after any job interview. And, frankly, most of us are looking to communicate that kind of personal brand, right? So, take a moment to read through each one of these Busters, think about them, and be honest with yourself. Have you fallen prey to any of these habits during your own job search?

Now, let's bust those Busters!

---

* Job-Seeker Personal Brand Busters™ and Job-Seeker Personal Brand Boosters™ are part of the Personal Brand Busters™ Series. For more information on other career and on-the-job Busters, visit www.HowYOUAreLikeShampoo.com.

19

Quiz: The Top 20 Job-Seeker Personal Brand Busters™

I never make stupid mistakes. Only very, very clever ones.
— John Peel, British broadcaster

Mistakes aren't stupid unless we don't learn from them. In fact, I side with Peel: Most mistakes are actually "very, very clever" because they open doors to help us get better and better at communicating our personal brands.

As we said in the previous chapter, that's what Job-Seeker Personal Brand Busters™ are all about — the mistakes others have made during a job search that we can all learn from and avoid. If you keep them top of mind, they can keep you from damaging your own job-seeker personal brand. They are the pitfalls and traps to watch out for as you start to put your Job-Seeker Personal Brand Marketing Plan into action.

Through my interviews with human resources managers and recruiting experts from companies all over the world, I have compiled the top 20 most damaging Job-Seeker Personal Brand Busters™. They are divided into our five Job-Seeker Marketing Plan Activities: Actions, Reactions, Look, Sound, and Thoughts — four Busters each. Do you recognize yourself in any of these? After you have finished reading them, take the quiz located at the end of this chapter, and test yourself on these Busters. How well do you score? You will then know exactly what to avoid as you progress through your job search and stay on your toes during every interview.

Job-Seeker Personal Brand Busters™—Actions

1. **Lying on your resume or during an interview.** Studies show that a large number of people actually lie on their resumes. These lies range from exaggerating experience to actually falsifying "facts" — like a job title or dates of employment — that can be easily checked out by a potential employer.

   When asked why, most job seekers say: "Come on — one little white lie won't hurt, will it?" Well, according to every single one of the experts I spoke with, it could hurt a lot — especially since computer technology has made it so much easier and quicker to check credentials. The potential result of lying on your resume? Someone is almost certain to discover it eventually. If the lie is uncovered before your interview, you won't get the interview at all. If the truth comes out after your interview, you won't get the job. And, if you're found out after you get the job, well, frankly, there's a good chance you'll be fired. Just try explaining *that* to your next interviewer.

   It's normal to use your resume or an interview to frame any potential negatives in as positive a light as possible, but making up experiences or lying about something, like your education, will get you nowhere. There is 0% upside and 100% potential downside. Even if the lie feels "unimportant," people will view you as dishonest if you're caught. And who wants to hire somebody with a dishonest personal brand? Erin Padilla of Talent Plus explains it like this: "Lying on your resume says to an employer that you have bad integrity. Believe me, word will spread in your field of work amongst colleagues."

   If you're remaining true to who you are, there's no reason to lie, and you'll be hired because of what YOU™ have to offer. It also just feels better knowing that you're living a life of integrity. Out of that comes a greater sense of fulfillment and, when you're consistently honest with yourself and others, your self-esteem increases, too. So, putting it frankly, lying on your resume is a lose-lose situation. Bottom line: Just don't do it.

2. **Asking questions about pay and benefits during an initial interview.** Recruiters tell me they immediately read that kind

of question as a sign of someone with little experience. On top of that, it gives the impression that you're more interested in what the employer can do for you than what you can do for the employer. Don't forget that your *Audience's* Needs are key to success in personal branding! Asking about pay in your first meeting may also make your interviewer think that you'll leave before long because you'll always be looking for the next better-paying job. So, while you should feel free to ask an employment agent or recruiter about salary and benefits, don't ask it when you're actually in an initial interview with a potential company. Michelle Lederman of Executive Essentials says: "It sends a signal that all you care about is the money. No company wants to hire someone who's interested in nothing but how big of a paycheck comes along with the job."

Before asking about the particulars of salary, etc., make sure the company and the job are a good fit for YOU™. Don't get me wrong: You definitely have every right to know what a company has to offer you eventually, but an initial interview isn't the right time to ask about salary or benefits unless the interviewer brings it up. When the company finally makes you an offer, that's when you can get more specific about salary and benefits. In the meantime, focus on showing the interviewer what a great contribution you can make to the company.

3. **Not performing a "trial run" to find out how long it takes to get from home to the interview site.** Don't run the risk of being late for your interview! Michelle Lederman says: "Showing up late shows a lack of planning and prioritizing of time." And that's definitely not a good job-seeker personal brand.

Even if you're on time, you don't want to be out of breath and dripping with sweat because you had to sprint the last 50 yards. So, a trial run is key. Make sure to do your trial run around the same time of day as the interview. If you're scheduled for an interview during rush hour traffic, a trial run during late morning hours won't give you a good sense of how much travel time you'll really need.

How about arriving early? Well, it's certainly better to arrive early than to arrive late, but if you do arrive early, Erin Padilla says: "Wait in the lobby or outside of the building until ten minutes before your scheduled meeting."

Of course, there might be times when you're late through no fault of your own. If that happens, apologize genuinely and explain that your being late was definitely beyond your control. Keep your excuse brief, however; protesting too much may come across as though you're not telling the truth!

4. **Not sending an immediate follow-up thank you to your interviewer.** This one is only important if you want to stand out from the pack! HR experts estimate that only about 10% of all candidates ever send a follow-up thank you note, so make sure to do this. And don't just thank the interviewer for the meeting, but use your note to help show again how interested you are in the job. Point out why you think you'd be a great fit for the job and the company. Nora Bammann, Assistant Human Resources Manager of The Kroger Company, stresses that "interviewees should send a thank you to everyone with whom they interviewed. If the interviewee did not get contact information or business cards from each interviewer, then at least acknowledge the other interviewers, and ask the primary contact to extend your thanks/appreciation to the others on your behalf."

Should your thank you be sent via e-mail or snail mail? Today, most thank you notes will be sent by e-mail. If your interviewer told you that it will take a couple of weeks or more to make a decision, however, it may be to your advantage to send your thank you note in regular mail. Think about it: These days, people get more junk e-mail than snail mail. Your note may stand out more if it arrives in the hands of the mail carrier. Of course, send your note no later than the day immediately following your interview. If there's a possibility the company will make a decision quickly, don't take a chance: Send your thank you by e-mail right away.

Even if you don't think you'll get the job, send a thank you note anyway! Remember my story about the job I didn't get until after I'd sent my thank you note saying I'd like to be considered for future openings? My boss at that company later told me that when he received my thank you note, he knew in the pit of his stomach that he had made the wrong decision in hiring the other person. He said that my thank you note was so professional that he already knew the first person he hired wouldn't work out — and he was right! So, take that as an important lesson, and send that thank you note no matter what.

Job-Seeker Personal Brand Busters™—Reactions

1. **Not listening to the question and veering off into an unrelated topic.** When you're nervous in an interview, it's easy to get lost in your Thoughts. That's especially true if you're worried about something you just said, or if you find the interviewer a bit cool and unfriendly. But it's incredibly important to focus during an interview and really listen to what the interviewer is saying and the questions that are being asked.

   Why? Well, if your answer isn't really related to the question, the interviewer might take away from the meeting that you're someone who doesn't listen, and that can count against you. If, by chance, your mind wandered, and you lost track of the question, definitely ask the interviewer to repeat the question again. You'll have the opportunity to hear the question one more time — and this time, of course, listen carefully.

   If you know that you have a tendency to veer off of the topic, really focus on answering questions as directly as possible. Then … STOP. That helps guard you against going off on another subject or saying too much. Just answer the question to the best of your ability, and then, be quiet and wait for the next question.

   If, however, you think the question could be linked to something else that's relevant about your background or experience, it's okay to say, "Could I take a moment to share with you a related story that could give you a better understanding?" But make sure that the story truly is related to the original topic.

2. **Answering a question without taking the time to think or before fully understanding the question.** Let's say you're in an important interview, and you're asked a question that takes you by surprise. You're not sure how to respond, but you feel the need to say something right away in order to look confident. So, you just start babbling whatever comes to mind. Does this sound at all familiar? If so, here's an insight: Interviewers actually prefer you take a moment to think before answering a question. They'd rather have a moment of pause and a thoughtful response than a rushed answer to every question. And trust me: If you do rush to answer every question, you won't be at your best. In fact, you may end up saying something you don't really mean.

What if you need some time to reflect on a challenging question? It's perfectly okay to say, "That's an interesting question. Give me a minute to think about that." Of course, don't take a *full minute* to think of your answer. When you're sitting across from an interviewer, 60 seconds of silence can feel like an eternity! But you should feel free to take a few seconds to think of a good answer before you speak. You're bound to have a better answer than if you had just started talking without thinking.

3. **Letting a "trick question" fluster you.** Unfortunately, some interviewers ask tricky questions on purpose to see how an interviewee might react in a stressful situation. If this happens to you, there are a couple of tactics you can try. First, ask for clarification to make sure you understand the question. Then, take a moment to stop and think about what the best answer might be.

For example, the interviewer might ask you, "What would you say if I told you that your qualifications aren't really a good fit for this job?" One possible response might be to ask a clarifying question: "Can you help me understand better what you're looking for? Maybe there's something I haven't shared with you yet that will help you to see how I am qualified." The key is not to get defensive. Think about how you could turn this type of out-of-the-blue question into a "win" for you by playing up your strengths.

Another possible trick question is, "What are some of the things about your previous boss that you didn't like?" This kind of question can be a minefield, and the key to answering this is to be clear but diplomatic. If you've already mentioned you had problems with your former boss, focus on answering the question honestly without showing anger or putting anyone down. No matter what, you definitely want to avoid saying something personal about your former boss when faced with this type of question. For example, you might say something like, "I would have liked my former boss to really get our team engaged and motivated more often so that everyone really bought into what we were trying to achieve." In other words, say something smart and truthful but still fairly harmless.

4. **Taking too long to accept an offer.** Experts say that if you wait to respond to an offer for a day or two, a potential employer will wonder if you're still interested. Nora Bammann says: "Another pet peeve is not only taking too long, but asking for an extension of the deadline in which to respond!" If you do this, a potential employer will begin

to believe that you're using their offer to "leverage up" another offer from a different company. I saw this behavior frequently when I was getting ready to graduate from business school. Graduates would take existing job offers and use them to try to get the job they wanted most. It's a dangerous game that could tarnish your reputation and cause you to lose a great potential opportunity. When a company makes an offer, show respect and give your answer within 24 hours.

Job-Seeker Personal Brand Busters™—Look

1. **Appearing tense and "tight" during an interview.** Do your shoulders get tight and rigid when you're nervous? Does your jaw clench, or do your eyes blink rapidly? Do you tend to clutch the arms of your chair without realizing it? Begin to become aware if any of these signs of nervousness are a problem for you. Then, get busy learning how to relax.

Before your interview, do some neck rolls to loosen your muscles. Try raising your shoulders up to your ears and then releasing them a couple of times. Use the tips from the Actions chapter (Chapter 12), and practice calming yourself both physically and emotionally before you arrive at the interview.

If you enter the interviewer's office with a smile on your face and with your arm extended out from your body for a friendly handshake, you will immediately feel better and more open.

Even if your body appears relaxed, you may still come across as tense as a result of what you say. For example, if the interviewer starts off the interview with "So, tell me about yourself," don't say "My name is _____, and I graduated from _____." If you "talk" your resume rather than begin a true dialogue with the interviewer, you run the risk of coming across rigid and less than confident. Simply respond to this question as naturally as possible, outlining your passions, Unique Strengths, and how you think your skills are a good fit for the company and the job.

If an opportunity opens up for some small talk, take it. Say something about the décor of the offices if you especially like the design, or simply say: "I really appreciate you seeing me today. I've been looking forward to meeting you and learning more about the company." Even just making a relaxed comment like that will help to calm you down for the remainder of the interview.

2. **Not visiting the restroom prior to your interview.** Let's get the obvious out of the way: You definitely don't want to squirm in your chair because you haven't had time to go to the restroom before the interview! But you should also use a quick pop into the restroom to check your appearance in the mirror before heading into an interview. Has the wind undone your "do"? Do you have lint on your suit? Is your tie crooked? Do you have a spot of dirt on your face? Even if nothing needs to be fixed, you will feel better knowing that YOU™ look your best.

3. **Only looking at one interviewer when there are two or more interviewers present.** People tend to look at the person who is most expressive or seems the most receptive. But if you're interviewed by more than one person, make sure you look at everyone in the room when you speak. Make eye contact with one interviewer for a few seconds; then, shift to another. If you don't, the interviewers you ignore may not connect with you. It's simply human nature.

4. **Not paying attention to YOU™ on the Internet.** Chances are your interviewer or future boss will do a "Google search" on you prior to your interview. If you're not careful, a search like that could actually prevent you from even getting an interview! The "Look" of YOU™ on the Internet could hurt your personal brand in a number of ways. Think twice before posting those wild photos from last year's Mardi Gras on your Facebook page or a picture of you passed out on your friend's living room couch on your Myspace page. If you blog or use Twitter, pay attention to what you say. Avoid negative comments about other people (especially former employers and co-workers), and steer away from profanity, strong controversial opinions about politics, or potentially embarrassing personal information about you or anyone else. Remember: Privacy is virtually non-existent on the Internet. As soon as you post it, your secret is out, and you may unconsciously damage your job-seeker personal brand faster than you can click your mouse!

Job-Seeker Personal Brand Busters™—Sound

1. **Talking only about what *you* want out of the job and not what the company needs or wants.** Make sure you focus on your Audience's Needs in the interview. Initially, the employer is more interested in what you can do for the company and not vice versa. If you're asked in the interview what you want from the job, answer the question

intelligently, but don't go on and on about all that you're hoping the company can offer you. The interview is your chance to show what *you* can offer the company so that the employer will want to hire you. Focus on highlighting your Unique Strengths, Reasons Why, and Brand Character traits and how they would be a great match for the specific job, as well as for the company as a whole.

2. **Not being prepared with good, thoughtful questions to ask at the end of an interview.** Being prepared with smart questions will show not only that you did your research but that you really gave some thought as to how you could fit into the company. It will also show that you're listening to the interviewer. And paying close attention to what is being said in the interview also helps you to ask a related question at the end. Nora Bammann says: "*Always* have questions ready. The questions interviewees ask really tell me (a) how the interviewee processes the information they heard, and (b) if the interviewee was not only listening but if they understood what they heard." So, have some questions prepared, but also feel free to ask questions in the moment based on what you're told by the interviewer. It shows you want to be a part of the organization and that you're taking the process seriously. If you need help thinking of questions to ask the interviewer, check out Appendix A for ideas.

3. **Not asking questions that will help you sell yourself.** Ask questions in a way that highlights your strengths. Here are some examples of the way you can ask a question that actually helps sell YOU™ in an interview:

   - "Given my experience managing big projects in my current job, do you see opportunities for someone like me to take on a project manager role here, too?"

   - "I've been giving some thought to how I might help sell the services your company offers. I've used a number of unique approaches in the past that worked well in my former job. How open is the company to exploring new ideas like this?"

Keep in mind: The questions you ask are often the last thing that happens in an interview. Just like the first impression counts, so does the "last" impression because it may be what the interviewer remembers most about you. So, a well-placed question or two at the end of an interview can leave the interviewer with a positive image of YOU™.

4. **Speaking negatively about your current or former employer.** In a survey of interviewers and recruiters conducted by CareerBuilders.com, 49% said that the worst interview offense is speaking negatively about a former boss. This means that there must be a lot of job seekers out there committing this Job-Seeker Personal Brand Buster™! An interview is absolutely not the right time to air your grievances. Saying something mean-spirited about a former employer will leave a bad taste in an interviewer's mouth and may just make them wonder if you'll say similar things about them behind their back if they hire you. Negativity breeds negativity. Find a way to shed some positive light on your current or former company and boss. Take the high road with a glass that is always half full.

Job-Seeker Personal Brand Busters™—Thoughts

1. **Beating yourself up if you don't do well in an interview or if you don't get the job.** It makes no sense to jump to conclusions. First of all, you may have done better in the interview than you think, and the company's reasons for not choosing you may not have anything to do with you at all. For example, the company might have decided to eliminate the position entirely, or they may have chosen someone from within the company.

   Whatever you do, don't allow your Thoughts to become negative. It will only get you down and make the interview process more difficult. Review the Thoughts chapter for productive ways to handle a disappointment.

2. **Thinking of yourself as inferior to the interviewer.** Little will make you more anxious than believing the interviewer is more important or somehow "better" than you. If you're prone to feeling intimidated in interviews, give yourself a pep talk prior to walking into the company's building. Make a list of all of your accomplishments, and remind yourself what you have to offer the company. No matter what someone has accomplished, they are no "better" than you. Never diminish your value — either personally or professionally. Remember: The interview is just two people who want the same thing — to find the best person for the job. Think of the interview as a two-way conversation, not an audition or Judgment Day.

3. **Not staying optimistic.** The power of positive thinking is no joke, especially when it comes to interviewing and finding a new job. Even

if you don't feel inferior to the interviewer, giving yourself a pep talk prior to an interview is a great habit to adopt. Take the time to remind yourself of all you've achieved. Remember: The interviewer wants to like you and wants you to succeed just as much as you do! It makes an interviewer's job easier when they find the perfect person for the job, and the interview is your opportunity to show why you are that perfect fit.

Besides, evidence shows that optimists live longer and are more successful than pessimists, not to mention happier and more peaceful. All it requires is a mind shift. *Expect* good things to happen to you, and they will.

4. **Thinking that you can "wing it" when it comes to preparing for an interview.** Walking into an interview unprepared is a good way to blow it. Remember what we said in the Audience chapter? You need to know everything you can about the company and the interviewer, and you need to be prepared with answers and questions based on your Audience's Needs, your Unique Strengths, your Reasons Why, and your Brand Character traits. So, practice, practice, practice! Rehearsing is guaranteed to help you when it comes time for "the real deal." You'll feel more confident, and you won't be easily thrown by the questions that come your way. This is the way you get the job you want.

The Quiz

So, what Job-Seeker Personal Brand Busters™ do *you* need to bust? On the next page is a quiz to help you better understand how YOU™ do in interviews with our top 20 most damaging Job-Seeker Personal Brand Busters™. If you think you commit a particular Job-Seeker Personal Brand Buster™ at least 50% of the time or more, mark it "yes." If you think you commit that particular Buster less than 50% of the time, mark it "no."

At the end of the quiz is a key to score your answers. When you're finished, you'll have a very clear idea of how much work you need to do to keep from damaging your personal brand before, during, and after job interviews. But even if your score is a bit disappointing, take heart. As author F. Wikzek has said, "If you don't make mistakes, you're not working on hard enough problems. And *that's* a big mistake."

No matter your score, with this book and the *How YOU™ are like Shampoo for Job Seekers* personal branding system, you have a roadmap for getting your personal brand in shape for a job search like never before. Don't dwell on the past. Think in terms of what you will do from this moment on to make things better. After each Buster, jot down action steps that you will take to truly bust that particular Buster. What will you do to make sure you don't commit that Buster again?

Are you ready to take your quiz? Remember — be honest!

Quiz

Do You Occasionally Commit These Job-Seeker Personal Brand Busters™?

	Actions

Yes	No		Action Steps
☐	☐	1. Lying on your resume or during an interview.	
☐	☐	2. Asking questions about pay and benefits during an initial interview.	
☐	☐	3. Not performing a "trial run" to find out how long it takes to get from home to the interview site.	
☐	☐	4. Not sending an immediate follow-up thank you to your interviewer.	

Reactions

Yes	No		Action Steps
☐	☐	5. Not listening to the question and veering off into an unrelated topic.	
☐	☐	6. Answering a question without taking the time to think or before fully understanding the question.	
☐	☐	7. Letting a "trick question" fluster you.	
☐	☐	8. Taking too long to accept an offer.	

Look

Yes	No		Action Steps
☐	☐	9. Appearing tense and "tight" during an interview.	
☐	☐	10. Not visiting the restroom prior to your interview.	
☐	☐	11. Only looking at one interviewer when there are two or more interviewers present.	
☐	☐	12. Not paying attention to YOU™ on the internet.	

Sound

Yes	No		Action Steps
☐	☐	13. Talking only about what *you* want out of the job and not what the company needs or wants.	
☐	☐	14. Not being prepared with good, thoughtful questions to ask at the end of the interview.	
☐	☐	15. Not asking questions that will help you sell yourself.	
☐	☐	16. Speaking negatively about your current or former employer.	

Thoughts

Yes	No		Action Steps
☐	☐	17. Beating yourself up if you don't do well in an interview or if you don't get the job.	
☐	☐	18. Thinking of yourself as inferior to the interviewer.	
☐	☐	19. Not staying optimistic.	
☐	☐	20. Thinking that you can "wing it" when it comes to preparing for an interview.	

Scoring Your Job-Seeker Personal Brand Busters™ Quiz

Now, it's time to check out your score. Count the number of times you responded "yes," and compare your final number against this Job-Seeker Personal Brand Busters™ scorecard.

If the number of "yes" responses you gave is…

0 to 5   Well done! You're obviously a strong job-seeking personal brand builder. Keep up the good work, and don't stop until you have zero "yes" responses.

6 to 10   Choose one or two areas which you think could make the biggest difference in your job-seeker personal brand image, and set up a plan to focus on changing those behaviors in your upcoming job interviews.

11 to 20   The good news is: You've uncovered a number of opportunities to strengthen how well you communicate your personal brand throughout your job search. Identify three to four areas where you want to focus in the near future. Then, find a mentor or coach to provide feedback and encouragement along the way as you work on changing your job-seeker personal brand image before, during, and after interviews. It's never too late to change your personal brand. Bravo to you for taking the first step!

So, how did you do? Whatever your score on the quiz, I tip my hat to you because you have done a lot of work toward making your job-seeker personal brand a reality and toward getting a new position that will fulfill and excite you. Now, let's make sure you take the steps necessary to guarantee you will be successful at building your personal brand long-term. There's no need to leave anything to chance.

The Proven Pathway to Getting YOU™ a Great Job

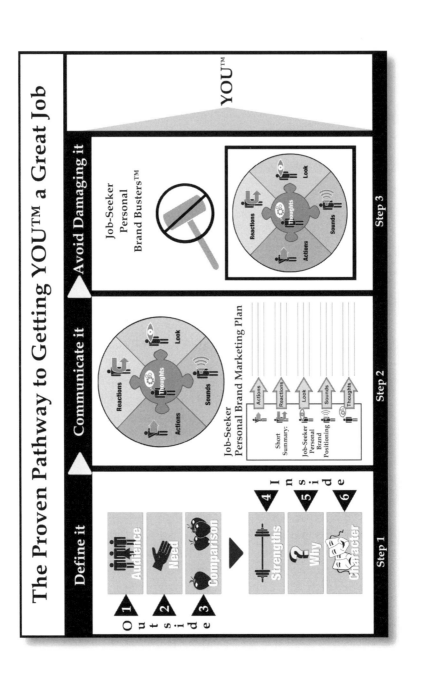

| Define it | Communicate it | Avoid Damaging it |

Define it

1 — Audience
2 — Need
3 — Comparison

Outside

4 — Strengths
5 — Why
6 — Character

Inside

Step 1

Communicate it

Look
Reactions
Thoughts
Actions
Sounds

Job-Seeker
Personal Brand Marketing Plan

Short Summary:

Job-Seeker Personal Brand Positioning

Actions
Reactions
Look
Sounds
Thoughts

Step 2

Avoid Damaging it

Job-Seeker
Personal
Brand Busters™

Look
Reactions
Thoughts
Actions
Sounds

Step 3

YOU™

20

Assuring
Long-Term Success

*I do not think that there is any other quality so essential
to success of any kind as the quality of perseverance. It
overcomes almost everything, even nature.*

— John D. Rockefeller, U.S. industrialist
and philanthropist

A s we near the end of this journey, it's a good idea to sit back and reflect on just how far you've come in developing your own unique job-seeker personal brand called YOU™. Together, we have applied this unique personal branding system to help you develop an individual personal brand that you can apply to a successful job search. We have:

- Looked at what personal branding is and what impact it can have on your ability to find and keep the best job for you.

- Defined the six core elements that make up your job-seeker personal brand — Audience, Need, Comparison, Unique Strengths, Reasons Why, and Brand Character — and we've pulled these elements together to create your distinctive and unique Job-Seeker Personal Brand Positioning Statement.

- Explored how to best communicate your job-seeker personal brand through the five activities that most impact how potential employers perceive, think, and feel about YOU™: Your Actions, your Reactions, your Look, your Sound, and your Thoughts.

- Developed a Job-Seeker Personal Brand Marketing Plan specific to YOU™ that outlines the Actions, Reactions, Look, Sound, and Thoughts you will adopt to make sure YOU™ come across consistently before, during, and after your interviews.

- Reviewed how to avoid harming your personal brand by watching out for key Job-Seeker Personal Brand Busters™ — including the top 20 most damaging Busters from our quiz as well as specific Busters from your own personal list.

Along the way, you've asked yourself and others some tough questions. You've had the chance to look at your job-seeker personal brand from an objective viewpoint. You've been able to craft a vision of your future in the job of your dreams. The bottom line is that you've become a great job-seeker personal brand builder, working toward building your brand with an Audience focus. Well done! All of this work will not only help you land the job you want, but can also help you develop a powerful personal brand in your new position that brings you greater opportunities for advancement and salary increases.

Of course, like any good marketer with a strong strategy, it isn't enough to simply have a plan. You have to follow through, sticking to that plan consistently — day in and day out.

Make Success a Done Deal

Be *confident* you can get the job you want within the company you like. A study done by the University of Washington found that participants who simply had more confidence in themselves were more likely to keep their New Year's resolutions. In other words, those participants who believed they could achieve their goals, did achieve them!

You're trying to create new habits and adopt new ways of behaving in interviews, so be both persistent and patient. If you make a mistake or two, don't beat yourself up. In that same University of Washington study, only 40% of the people who successfully achieved their top New Year's resolution did so on their first try. The rest tried several times, and 17% finally succeeded after more than six attempts. Persistence pays off, especially when it comes to looking for a job. Just learn from your mistakes to avoid spinning your wheels, and re-focus as fast as you can.

The work you have done to define and communicate your job-seeker personal brand will help you to stay committed to the vision of finding a great job. One idea to keep you focused is to develop a visual symbol that stands for your brand image. Keep it somewhere near you as a reminder, and look at it before you walk into an interview. You could put it in your pocket or your wallet on the same paper as your job-seeker personal brand summary so that you see or feel it every time you reach in for some money. Every time that symbol is brought to mind, you'll remember your personal brand objectives.

Find a trusted confidante to become your job-seeker personal brand buddy as you both look for jobs. You can help each other stay on track with your individual Job-Seeker Personal Brand Marketing Plans and support each other along the way. If you can't find a buddy to help you, consider hiring a coach or finding a mentor, if possible, to guide you during your job search. That kind of outside, objective perspective can be priceless.

Evolve Your Personal Brand

As human beings, we're not static, nor are we supposed to be. After you've successfully used your job-seeker personal brand to get the job you desire, you'll want to make adjustments to your brand. It will become your "on-the-job" brand which caters to your new company's Needs. This is where the first book in the YOU™ series — *How YOU™ are like Shampoo* — can help you in developing your personal brand for your new position. So, your personal brand will continue to grow and evolve over time, just as your favorite name brands evolve.

Remember when Apple only stood for the Macintosh computer? Now, Apple stands for much, much more. It has evolved its brand considerably in the past few years. In contrast, perhaps you can remember brands like Kodak, which hung its hat on film and took too long to respond to the growing digital camera trend. That's a brand that didn't evolve as quickly as it should have.

Just like these name brands, you have to evolve your own personal brand to fit with the changes that are happening around you. Once you get a new job (and any time you change jobs after that), you will want to create a Personal Brand Positioning Statement based on new information. Even if you stay in the same job for a long time, your brand will change as circumstances around you and within the company change. Stay alert for how those changes — such as a new boss or new focus in the company — might mean that parts of your personal brand need to be adjusted.

My Personal Note to YOU™

What a trip it's been to ride along with you on this road toward your job-seeker personal brand — YOU™! I hope to hear from you with regard to your job search successes, challenges, and questions as you build your Job-Seeker Personal Brand Positioning Statement and put your Job-Seeker Personal Brand Marketing Plan into action. Please write me at Brenda@BrendaBence.com. I would love to hear how your employment search is going and how the *How YOU™ are like Shampoo For Job Seekers* personal branding system helped you land a great job.

Also, please check out our online coaching modules for any help you might want along the way. Visit us at HowYOUAreLikeShampoo.com for more information.

Congratulations on taking control of your career success by learning to craft and communicate your job-seeker personal brand. I wish nothing less than the perfect job for YOU™, a lifetime of fulfillment, and great achievements along the way.

Appendix A

Great Interview Questions for YOU™

Thank you to Sigmund Ginsburg, Executive Search Consultant at the New York office of DHR International, for sharing this great list of questions to prepare for any interview.

Twenty Questions Coming Your Way

To ace an interview, nothing beats preparation. Here are 20 questions you'll want to be ready to answer.

1. Why did you decide to become a candidate for this position?

2. What do you see as this position's major challenges and opportunities — and its major difficulties and risks?

3. From what you know at this point about the position and the company, what appeals to you most? What do you like least?

4. When you leave this position, what would you like to be remembered for? And when you retire and end your career, what would you like people to say about you?

5. What do you see as your job after this one; what is your ultimate career goal?

6. What do you regard as your five major achievements in your life? … in your career?

7. What do you like best about your current position—what do you like least?

8. What decisions or actions have disappointed you in your career? If you had a chance to change them, what would you do instead?

9. Describe the most difficult supervisory problem you have had to deal with in your present job and how you handled it (if applicable).

10. How do you deal with the personal stress and/or the stressful situations that you experience on the job? How do you deal with subordinates, peers, and superiors who appear to be stressed?

11. At our company, we are currently facing or will face the following problem. Explain how you'd develop a process for dealing with this challenge and what you would anticipate as the outcome.

12. How have your present and past positions prepared you to take on the responsibilities of this position?

13. If we asked people who know you well to describe you, what five words would most frequently come up? What three reasons would they give as to why we should hire you?

14. If your supervisor sent you to represent your company at a very important meeting with people you have never met, what would he or she caution you about in terms of your style and approach to ensure that you would be an effective participant in the meeting?

15. Give us an example of a major crisis or chaotic situation you faced and what you did to manage it.

16. For what have you been most frequently praised — and most frequently criticized?

17. Suggest two or three qualities or characteristics that you believe would make you stand out in a crowd of excellent candidates.

18. If you could wave a magic wand so that this position turned out to be your dream job, what specific things would you want the wand to ensure?

19. What do you like to do when not working?

20. What would you want us to remember most about this interview?

A Dozen Queries to Pose

Here are 12 great questions you can ask any interviewer during an interview.

1. What are the major challenges, opportunities, risks, and minefields of the position?

2. Why is the job vacant, and what is the history of the position and of those who have held it?

3. How do management and others in the department regard this position?

4. What is the climate and culture of the company? Describe the typical working relationships between and among individuals, departments, and divisions (if applicable).

5. What have been the company's strategic plan priorities and to what degree have they been achieved?

6. What have been recent results of the company's _____ efforts? [Note: this question can be tailored to whatever you uncover in your sleuthing efforts. For example, perhaps the company is focusing on recruiting and retention.]

7. What type of managerial and personal style is likely to be effective in meeting the responsibilities of the position?

8. What is it like to work here?

9. Why should a candidate be seriously interested in the position and the company?

10. What current or potential negatives or concerns should I know about the position and the company?

11. How, after a year, would you assess whether you had made an excellent decision in selecting a candidate; what would you expect to have been accomplished? And what would that expectation be after three years?

12. What interests you most about me; what do you think I might be able to accomplish and contribute? What about me might cause you concern?

Appendix B

Personality Profiles and Tests

Assessment.com

www.assessment.com

MAPP is a personal assessment that takes about 15 minutes to complete. MAPP identifies your true motivations toward work and allows you to match yourself to job categories to see where you best fit. It's been used by job seekers, companies, schools, workforce centers and coaches. Job seekers wanting to learn more about their strengths and motivations toward work can take the MAPP assessment and receive a free sample report of their top motivators and job areas. If you like what you see, you can choose to purchase a full report. There are four options with retail prices ranging from $19.95 to $129.95 (for the full executive package). You can view report options and choose the best one for you.

Careering Ahead

www.careeringahead.com.au

Free. Out of Australia, this is a secured, online psychometric test. Self-described as a "simple and user-friendly process to make taking a psychometric test an enjoyable experience," the firm recommends you take the psychometric test in a quiet place and make sure you are undisturbed during this process.

The test is thorough and has about 4oo questions. It's helpful if you're unsure as to which direction to go in your career. The test gets you thinking more broadly, but allows you to narrow down to what is most important to you in your career.

Keirsey

www.keirsey.com

Retail Price: $19.95. Check out the Career Temperament Report which assists career professionals, job seekers, and students in the career exploration process. This report is designed to help people align their career preparation and choices with their innate strengths and preferences. It includes expert advice on career options, tips on communication / interpersonal skills, and insight on navigating the job market based on personality type. The Temperament Report provides suggested career matches based on research surveys conducted across a wide spectrum of industry.

Personality 100
www.personality100.com

PHD-certified personality test based on 60 years of research and three years of analysis. The questionnaire measures 32 dimensions. According to the website, millions have taken the test — which is free — but getting the results costs $29.95. Once you pay, you receive 100 pages of feedback, "objective and scientific."

Similarminds
www.similarminds.com

Free. Provides various tests such as 16 Type Jung Personality Tests, Personality Disorder Test, Compatibility Test, Career Test, Personality Test, Intelligence Test, etc. After you take a test, it provides instant feedback, usually in the form of a brief paragraph.

Strengths Finder
www.strengthsfinder.com

After you purchase the book *Now, Discover Your Strengths,* there is a code inside which allows you to access the StrengthsFinder online.

Gallup introduced the first version of its online assessment, StrengthsFinder, in the 2001 management book, *Now, Discover Your Strengths.* In StrengthsFinder 2.0, Gallup unveils the new and improved version of its popular assessment, Language of 34 Themes, and much more. You can read the book in one sitting, but they say "you'll use it as a reference for decades." These highly customized Strengths Insights will help you understand how each of your top five themes plays out in your life on a much more personal and professional level. The Strengths Insights describe what makes you stand out when compared to the millions of people that Gallup has studied.

This information, while verified and correct at the time of printing, is subject to change at any time. Please contact each provider directly to inquire about current tests and pricing. Thank you!

Suggested Books

Creating Brand Loyalty by Richard D. Czerniawski & Michael W. Maloney

Now, Discover Your Strengths by Marcus Buckingham & Donald O. Clifton, Ph.D.

The Definitive Book of Body Language by Barbara Pease and Allan Pease

Acting the Interview: How to Ask and Answer the Questions That Will Get You the Job! by Tony Beshara

Best Answers to the 201 Most Frequently Asked Interview Questions by Matthew J. Deluca

A Course in Miracles by Foundation for Inner Peace

About the Author

Brenda S. Bence is Founder and President of BDA (Brand Development Associates) International Ltd, a firm that specializes in helping companies and individual clients around the world build successful, growth-oriented corporate and personal brands. As an international speaker, trainer, executive coach, and consultant, Brenda has worked with hundreds of executives, managers, and entrepreneurs around

the world to help them define and communicate their corporate and personal brands. Brenda spends the majority of the year traveling to present her unique approach to branding at conferences, conventions, and corporations all across the globe.

Brenda earned an MBA from Harvard Business School and began her career as a marketer at Procter & Gamble, first at P&G's world headquarters in the U.S., then with P&G in Europe and in Asia. Subsequently, Brenda held the position of Vice President International Marketing for Bristol-Myers Squibb's consumer division, Mead Johnson, where she was responsible for multiple brands across almost 50 countries.

During her 25-year career, Brenda has helped manage dozens of well-known brands, including Pantene, Vidal Sassoon Shampoo & Styling products, Head & Shoulders, Enfamil, Choc-o-Milk, and Ariel and Cheer Laundry Detergents, just to name a few.

Brenda has an Honorary Doctor of Laws degree as well as a Bachelor of Arts degree in English and French from Nebraska Wesleyan University. She splits her time between homes in Thailand and the U.S. and sits on a number of boards of public and private companies and not-for-profit organizations. Brenda is a member of the International Federation for Professional Speakers (IFFPS) and Asia Professional Speakers (APS). Brenda is a Certified Coach with Results™ Coaching Systems and has earned the designation of Associate Certified Coach with the International Coach Federation.

Brenda has been happily married to her husband, Daniel, for over ten years. And she really *does* prefer him over her favorite toothpaste brand.

DRESS FOR SUCCESS®
Suits to Self-Sufficiency

Dress for Success® is an international non-profit organization dedicated to improving the lives of disadvantaged women. The professional clothing, employment retention programs, and ongoing support that Dress for Success provides its clients symbolize their faith in every woman's ability to be self-sufficient and successful in her career.

Founded in New York City in 1997 as an answer to the needs of low-income women who are seeking employment and self-sufficiency, Dress for Success is a 501(c)(3) not-for-profit organization. In the same year that Dress for Success was founded, the welfare overhaul set time restrictions for public assistance recipients, which in turn quickly forced heads of households into low wage jobs. Because of the rapid increase in the number of poor working women, they became an underserved segment of society, and many lacked the skills and support to retain their employment. Dress for Success has responded to the needs of the women that they serve by providing professional attire, career development tools, and a network of support to help women succeed in work and in life.

Over the past 11 years, Dress for Success has grown into a thriving international not-for-profit organization that has supported more than 450,000 disadvantaged women at over 90 affiliates worldwide. Dress for Success serves more than 30,000 clients each year throughout the United States, Canada, Mexico, Poland, New Zealand, the Netherlands, and the United Kingdom.

To make a donation, you may contact Dress for Success, 32 East 31st Street, 7th Floor, New York, NY 10016, or gift online at www.DressForSucess.org.

By way of support for this strong cause, author Brenda Bence and her husband, Daniel, have agreed to donate $1.00 to Dress for Success for every copy sold of the *How YOU*™ *are like Shampoo* series of personal branding books.

Acknowledgments

Writing is easy: All you do is sit staring at a blank sheet of paper until drops of blood form on your forehead.
— Gene Fowler

Writing really is a labor of love. And, as with any book, it is never just one person who makes it happen. Thank you to so many who have offered their incredible talents to turn this — my second — book from a Thought into reality. Sincere thanks go to:

- Melanie Votaw, editor extraordinaire, whose partnership I have enjoyed immensely
- Eric Myhr for his eagle-eye and outstanding typesetting services
- Graham Dixhorn for his great attitude and cover copywriting skills
- George Foster for terrific cover design and consistent willingness to try something new
- Brooke Deffenbaugh-Mullen for her thorough research assistance
- Kurt Heck for his photographic creativity
- Swas Siripong "Kwan" for great graphic design

I am most grateful to my job-seeker coaching clients for allowing me to ride along beside them on their journeys of discovery. Without them, this book would not have been possible.

I also owe a debt of gratitude to so many human resources experts from around the globe who helped me with input to the book and who patiently answered my incessant questions. There have been — literally — dozens who have helped me, but here are the folks who were the short-straw recipients of the bulk of my questions: Gary Woollacott of Opus Recruitment, Charles Moore of Heidrick & Struggles, Nora Bammann from The Kroger Company, Sumittra Meesuwan from MSD (Thailand) Ltd., Liz Handlin of Ultimate-Resumes.com, Michelle Lederman of Executive Essentials, Erin Padilla of Talent Plus, Yolanda Sing, formerly of MasterCard.

Besides those who actually worked "on" the book, there were a great many people who have been cheering me on during the months it took to develop this book. My sincere gratitude goes to:

Daniel, my consistently-supportive husband and business partner. You make me a better person and still manage to crack me up every single day.

Kathie and Danielle, for always helping me to see life through grounded eyes and for giving me honest feedback when you know I need it.

Khun Ruampon Panswad (Muk) and Khun Panita Sastrawaha (Tun), Executive Assistants at BDA International, for always being willing to do whatever the job takes … and still smile about it.

The entire staff at BDA International for their unwavering support and patience during months of writing and book development.

To My Team. You guys are great.

Brenda S. Bence

Professional Speaker, Trainer, and Coach

Motivate your team to greater workplace success by hiring Brenda to speak at an upcoming meeting or conference. Brenda Bence is in demand as a speaker not only for her unique approach to personal branding and marketing, but also for her warm, humorous, and entertaining personality. Her popular keynote addresses about personal branding draw on Brenda's decades of experience as a marketer and coach and help audiences to discover and leverage the core elements of her groundbreaking personal branding system. Through her practical, no-nonsense approach to personal branding, Brenda has guided and motivated employees and employers around the world to greater success in the workplace as well as to greater career fulfillment.

Empower your teams to greater success by hiring Brenda to conduct an in-house personal branding workshop. For organizations who would like to give their employees, staff, or teams more hands-on experience applying personal branding in the workplace, Brenda offers personal branding workshops which walk each participant through the Personal Brand Positioning Statement development process, as well as through the creation of participants' own at-work Personal Brand Marketing Plans. Brenda completes her workshops by helping participants uncover common Personal Brand Busters™ — the personal branding mistakes they may be making themselves on the job or mistakes that others have made before them. Attending one of Brenda's workshops leaves participants with a clear and practical formula for success at work through personal branding.

Achieve greater personal career success by hiring Brenda as your own executive coach. For leaders who would like one-on-one assistance in developing and communicating their personal brands on the job, Brenda offers in-person and telephone coaching for CEOs, Senior Executives, Senior Managers, and Business Owners located anywhere in the world. Trained in the Results™ Professional Coaching method, Brenda's approach is much like having a partner "running alongside you" at work, giving you perspective and encouragement as you put your leadership personal brand into action. Just as a personal trainer helps you craft a plan to reach pre-defined fitness goals and stretches you to reach those goals, Brenda works with you to think *bigger* and then, helps you to break down your new "big" goals into actionable tasks that lead you toward success.

To book Brenda Bence as a speaker or trainer at your next conference, convention, or in-house event—or to arrange for coaching—please contact:

Telephone in North America (Chicago, U.S.A.):	1-312-214-4994
Facsimile in North America (Chicago, U.S.A.):	1-312-277-9211
Telephone in Asia (Bangkok, Thailand):	+662-627-9327
Facsimile in Asia (Bangkok, Thailand):	+662-711-9210

E-mail Brenda at:

Brenda@BrendaBence.com

To find out more about Brenda's programs, products, and clients, visit her website at:

www.BrendaBence.com

Brenda would love to hear how this book has impacted your job search, your career and your life. To share your personal brand stories, insights, and experiences with Brenda, e-mail:

Comments@BrendaBence.com

Web

Be sure to take advantage of the free personal branding tools and sign up for Brenda's personal branding e-newsletter at www.HowYOUAreLikeShampoo.com

Other Books and Products
by Brenda Bence

Paperback Book
How YOU™ are like Shampoo

The breakthrough Personal Branding System
based on proven big-brand marketing methods
to help you earn more, do more, and be more at work

Published in January 2008

Category:
- Best Book:
  Business/Career

5-CD Audio Book
How YOU™ are like Shampoo

The breakthrough Personal Branding System
based on proven big-brand marketing methods
to help you earn more, do more, and be more at work

Released in January 2008

Categories:
- Best Audio Book:
  Self-Help/Motivational
- Best Audio Book:
  Non-Fiction Unabridged

Audio Book is available in MP3 download format
Visit www.HowYOUAreLikeShampoo.com
for more information